CRYSTAL BEYOND THE CURTAIN

BY PATRICIA ANN GAMET

Dedication

This book is dedicated to the Father, His Son and Spirit. Crystal Beyond the Curtain is also dedicated to their "overcomers"' the "Army of Joel", who will do the "Greater Works" in the "End of Days."

Gloryrealm Productions
Copyright 2001 Patricia Gamet
ISBN 0 9 7 0 9 3 1 5-0-6
Production Manager: Elfin Cove Press

TABLE OF CONTENTS

PRELUDE

FOR MANY PEOPLE, LIFE IS A PRISON SENTENCE

We watch the destruction of our planet, and it seems sometimes that your life and other people's lives can feel dismal. Whether they are truly in jail or are in a prison of their own or another person's making, they are still captives. Let's be honest. Most of us at one time or another, or even now, are miserable! Life is not easy. But there truly is "good news." There is a shooting ray of light from heaven that is just about to flash into the "dark cells" of men's hearts and brilliantly light and overtake the darkness. It is the glory from above.

The Father is just about to explode in a "glory-shoot" of such magnitude on planet Earth that men will be utterly astounded. For a reviving restoration of those who sit in darkness is just a heartbeat away.

Things too wonderful are just around the corner for us. As God's Spirit is poured out upon a waiting planet and upon broken hearts, such unspeakable joy will be upon His People that it defies human words to tell of it.

I believe this book, Crystal Beyond the Curtain, is a forerunner of this coming "love-fest" that is just about to hit the earth.

For when heaven's curtain is drawn aside and we shall glimpse the Sardine Stone, Who sits upon His throne, Who speaks with the voice of many waters, we shall know how truly and totally we are loved. (Rev. 4: 3)

DAUGHTER, IN THE BEGINNING ...

when I made Adam and Eve and they fell through sin, I knew that My People would suffer. My pain was that I would watch and not be able to help, like I wanted to. But then Jesus, My Son, came into the earth and brought man from death to life. Still, man suffered, but at least the human race had hope.

I see your suffering and feel your pain. Oh yes, I feel man's pain. You and I have been one since you were a little girl. I never left you when you left Me. I've always been with you. I've watched your progress since before the womb and after. I see what your days have been. And I say now, too, "Let no man hurt you." For in so doing, he will bring damnation on himself.

You are My voice in the earth and more. You will fulfill other ministries for Me. And I say, "My 'voice,' you will be pure." When men say evil against you, they say evil against Me. I say, "Let no man hurt or touch My Anointed, and no demon either." For I have raised you up, not man. "A bruised reed, I will not break." Satan thinks he's ready to move in for the kill, but he hasn't got a chance. He thinks he's nearly destroyed you, but I have news for him; you are ready to rise up and put him down. You shall be as the morning. Your light shall shine among men. You don't have to do anything except wait for the promise. And the waiting is coming to an end soon. You have waited your whole life. You have felt it in your spirit, too, always waiting, but you didn't know what you waited for. Soon, you will know.

I see you and feel your spirit upon your bed at night. I hear the inner weeping and moans of your spirit, although they don't show in the natural. I feel your deep longings and hear your silent screams of pain. I have felt them all, too, sweet one. I have seen you asleep at night on your bed and held you in My Heart and longed to hold you in My Arms. I have set special forces of angels around you to protect you, angels most people don't have. You were one of My Closest, Dearest Children before you left heaven. You had an extra special love for Me, a sacrificial love that most people don't have. Yes, you've seen correctly when you saw the counsel and when you saw yourself agreeing to do all I asked of you on the earth. What people haven't seen is that all the terrible illnesses, accidents, and life-threatening things in your life have been to destroy you so you couldn't accomplish what I have for you to do. You have tried to overcome the illnesses and have tried to fight with faith. No, you haven't been perfect, but a great battle in the heavens has been waged against you since your conception, not just your birth. You have walked the way of the cross of suffering, and people have criticized and judged you for it. No, you have not been perfect in your walk, but you have been in a battle zone all your days. Other people have had battles, but it's hard for them to know the measure of the pressures put upon you. They cannot conceive of another having worse battles than themselves, and they do not want to because it diminishes their own suffering. People have not really had the understanding of the areas you've walked in and the tremendous attacks on your life—not even you have known the full scale of the warfare to destroy you.

But take joy; I've overcome them all. I suffered when I watched Jesus—more than He did—just like an earthly father, and I've suffered more than you when you have suffered.

Yes, you have the heart of David. And I will exalt you as David. At the end of suffering is a reward—the fulfillment of the promise. I have had you reading Psalms for a purpose all these years. I wanted you to learn of David and Myself. I wanted to comfort you in your afflictions.

You will have an apostle's ministry and other ministries as well in the earth. You will walk among men and they will know you are My apostle. I have called you. Though men may not always receive you, remember these words that I speak this day. Let them be burned into your spirit.

This day, I would have you send out your angels to do battle against Satan's angels and fight a war against afflictions and infirmities.

I have given you a special army of angels this day, added to your forces, that, when the going gets tough, you can call upon for battle, ministering, and the calling down of special gifts. They'll never leave you again; use them.

Men will start to know you more and more, because this day I anoint you with a fresh anointing of oil that would go into your very spirit: the anointing of the fire-warrior, the prophet, apostle, and evangelist. You are branded this day with a new fire—spirit fire, a special unusual anointing that no man prays or bestows upon you, an anointing by God's Own Hand that what I want done on the earth will be done.

No, daughter, you aren't having delusions of grandeur as you fear, but I am telling you the truth. Do not worry— rejoice, for your strength draweth nigh.

(He gave me Mark 4:11: "And He said unto them, 'Unto you it is given to know the mystery of the Kingdom of God: but unto them that are without, all these things are done in parables'.")

THE PRINCESS AND THE PEA

I remember myself as a very young child with an almost detached feeling of love for the little girl I was. It's as if she was somehow another person that I can look back at with tenderness, and yet she and I are one. Her name was Patricia, which means "Royal One," and Ann, which means "Gracious One."

My mother was a beauty, full of life, with dark eyes that sparkled when she laughed. She was full of fun, yet very understanding and gentle. I was born with thick black hair, which was three or four inches long, and bright blue eyes. The nurse said when she brought me in for the first time to my mother that I was a very sensitive person because my little lip quivered when I became upset. She said she had seen other babies who had the same reaction and that they were always sensitive in nature. After my traumatic entrance into this cold world, it was no wonder my lip quivered. My father was an alcoholic. In spite of his problems, I loved him madly, as I did my mother.

Each life is a story written on the heart of God. He knows each moment, each event, of every person's life. He is always watching us, always stands ready to help us when we cry out to Him—no matter who we are or what acts of evil we have done. He rejects no man. He loves man. Only man rejects God. He feels our pain and His Own Pain, too, when He sees the sorrows of our lives. But He also rejoices when we overcome and succeed.

HAVE YOU EVER FELT THAT YOU HAVE BEEN WAITING FOR SOMETHING ...

for so long, but you didn't know what it was?

The Father knows, and He wants to "take you away," up, out of your world, and out of yourself. He wants to take you to another place: into the "Sea of Glory." He longs to immerse you in the "waters of love" and splash His Enraptured Spirit into yours.

He greatly desires to place the "Keys to the Kingdom" into your sweet hand so that you can unlock doors to heaven's realms. He wants to give you "new eyes."

Enter through the snowy white veil and gaze upon the "Crystal Sea that burns with Holy Fire." Dive in and let the effervescent glory-waters wash over you, bringing "fragrant new life" to your very being.

For even now, scarlet cords are being loosed by the "Ancient of Days." The scrolls are beginning to flutter and open, unveiling the secret mysteries reserved for this precise moment in the Heartbeat of God!

References: Song of Solomon 2: 10 Amplified Bible -My beloved speaks and says to me, "Rise up, my love, my fair one, and come away."
Revelation 22: 1 King James -And he shewed me a pure river of water of life, clear as crystal, proceeding out of the throne of God and of the Lamb.

FOREWORD

THE WORDS WRITTEN IN THIS BOOK ...

are meant to be simple and informal. They are written by the inspiration of the Father and creator of all peoples everywhere. The God of all the universe wants to be a friend to you. He wants to talk to you and listen to your thoughts. He wants to feel your pain and joy. He wants to laugh when you laugh and cry along with you when you are sad. He wants to be everything to you and longs to have you fall in love with Him.

If you are a homosexual, He loves you; if you are a murderer, He loves you still. If you are in the occult and practicing witchcraft, He loves you. If you have had or done abortions, He is here for you. If you have lied, cheated, stolen, been a prostitute or pimp, or done many perversions, He is still with you. Whatever your sin, His arms are wide open to you. He hates the sin, but loves you so much that He has given His Treasure for your heart. Don't ever turn from the One who longs for you. Many of you have never known true love. You have been hurt by those who should have loved you. He understands, because His Son was rejected and put to death by the very ones He came to help. The Father wants you to know, in spite of your disillusionment with people who have brought you so much pain, that He is not like mere humans. His love for you stretches across the heavens. His love is fathomless, limitless, and goes into the lowest sea and highest heaven. His love for you, sinful man and child of God, is beyond your comprehension, beyond man's mind.
His love is ... the very heart of God.

I HAVE BANGED MY HEAD
AGAINST THE WALL

trying to achieve financial success in my life and, more importantly, personal success that cries out, "I finally made it!" But much of my desire for great achievement had, at the root of it, what the Bible calls the "pride of life." Alas, my life had been filled with much frustration and embarrassment at not being what others would call truly successful. The Father gave me many talents, yet I could never really seem to succeed completely or accomplish the goals I longed to accomplish. Perhaps self-centeredness was also a root cause. Wanting to make my family and friends proud of me was also important. Yet, maybe I missed the point—that being that life is in the living and that the pot of gold at the end of the rainbow that I sought was there, buried in my life all along, waiting to be found in the ordinary day-to-day journey of life.

When I was five years old, a man asked me, "What do you want to do when you grow up?" I said, "I want to help people." He seemed amazed, I imagine, because of my young age. He congratulated me on my noble pursuit.

Yet on the path of my life, I strayed away from God after having been miraculously "saved" by Him personally in my room at a young age. I left him—He did not leave me—but still my life became a mess. Yet He brought me back to Himself tenderly. Through many grueling years, He sustained and helped me in spite of many "deep waters."

Now, I am writing to you about the One who has always been there for me as well as for you. Sometimes, we get mad at Him for things He actually did not do to us or to the people we love, but He understands our frailties in His Gentle Wisdom. You see, God gets the "bad rap" much of the time instead of our real enemy, Satan. God is not a baby slayer or a killer of those who perish in auto accidents or at the hands of violent people. He says, "Death is an enemy."

"The Thief comes to steal, kill, and destroy, but I have come that they might have life, and life more abundantly." Ultimately, man's sin has been the tool that has released Satan's ability to kill, steal, and destroy. All the while, the Father has been protecting and deflecting the enemy from our loved ones and us whenever He can. But God set up certain rules in the universe that even He must abide by, or He would be a liar and would perish. The basis of these is, "That which a man sows, so shall he reap." When there is sin, even back to the tenth generation, it opens doors in the Spirit Realm to the enemy through which he can steal, kill, and destroy. This is what happened when Adam and Eve sinned. They opened doors to horrendous evil. You say, "Not fair." But it is fair, because God is a Holy God; He had to have holy people. This is why God sent the serpent into Eden, so that He would find out what was truly in Adam's and Eve's hearts. For darkness and light cannot dwell together. The Father could not change His Holy and Pure Nature, for He says, "There is no shadow of turning in Him." He is the same yesterday, today, and forever. So to help man, He sent the One who was so precious and close to Him, His Son Ya'shua (Jesus). He would bring mankind from eternal death to life. The work was finished and complete. Yet man was still so spiritually ignorant that Satan could tempt him to sin, and in so doing, cause generational curses. Unsaved, man's heart was still corrupt without Jesus. And even those who did possess Jesus still needed to experience all that God had given them. The church has not really laid hold of what is rightfully hers: righteousness and being freed from the Law of Sin and Death. This is why, in the next few years, we shall see the greatest revival ever known to mankind. God will finally fulfill His promises to His people. The Servants of the Lord shall be completed and free and shall do the "greater works."

All eternity and all the angels in the heavens await the panorama about to unfold upon this earth. For soon, great darkness (spiritual darkness) shall cover the land, but "where there is the greatest darkness, there is the greatest light."

Soon, we will see Jesus and the Father and the Spirit revealed to man in a way never before seen by a human being. For they shall be seen in great splendor, glory, and astonishment by the nations and God's own.

INTRODUCTION

DEAR PEOPLES OF THE EARTH ...

and My Beloved Children, I want you to know, it is the Father who writes you these words, not a mortal. I have caused a woman to write these words for Me, so that you could get to know who I am. There have been many secrets that I have hidden from man for so long. Now the time is ripe to share these "pearls of great price" with people everywhere. I hope that you will revere these words and not mock them, for your own sakes. I do not have to tell you these things, but I do tell you them to help you. I am opening up My kingdom knowledge and Myself for the love of you.

There are days—very, very shortly ahead—where you will need to know these truths I tell you. The days that are coming soon are unimaginable! They will make the movies that you watch look like children's fairy tales, gentle and sweet. You are probably thinking, "Was The Terminator sweet and gentle? Was The Exorcist a sweet fairy tale?" And I say, "Yes, compared to what lies ahead, yes!" You see, the stage is now set for such an onslaught of evil this world has never begun to know or even imagine, because it is beyond even the evil capabilities of man; it is from the heart of Satan. The stage of earth is set. The play is ready to unfold with force. The curtain, the unveiling, is ready to open, and behind it are all manner of wild and wicked things. New and desperate terrors are ready to unfold upon a waiting world that is asleep to the "conspiracy of the ages." All that Satan has stored up in the pit of Hell, all his dark powers and forces, are about to be loosed onto a sleeping planet. For so few are really awake to what is coming! The Antichrist, the son of Hell, is in the wings. He is dressed and ready to walk boldly onto the stage of the earth. He will come as an angel of light, a great ruler of nations. He will appear to have all the answers to the desperation of the hour. He will speak "smooth things, wonderful things." People will be captivated by his charm and great intelligence. He will appear to be the great counselor and comforter to man. But lurking beside and inside him is the Evil One who longs to ultimately destroy what I have created—mankind. So do not be deceived by this wickedness incarnate, this Son of Perdition. Do not receive his mark, "The Mark of the Beast," on your body because then, I will count you as one of his forever. If you wonder, "How will I buy my food, clothing, shelter, my car, or how will I be able to sell or trade without the number that so many will be marked with?" I will tell you. I take care of My Own. I know you will fear for your children. I also know how to take care of you and your children. The answer to this problem is that you must give Me yourself—totally. Then I can take care of you and keep you safe in the days ahead.

I say this now with great sorrow in My Heart, not sorrow as you know it. Because you are human, you do not feel as I feel. You really cannot imagine what pain is like for Me. If you were to feel a small portion of the pain I feel for mankind, it would kill you, burn you up in an instant. So I only let people feel a minuscule amount of pain for their protection. My Heart is heavy, and the pain is so real and terrible for Me when I realize that many, many people will not turn to Me and will go down instead into the pit of Hell. There will be many Christians who will not come up into heaven with Me because they don't love Me enough. There will also be many Christians who will only be in heaven with Me through much suffering and eventual death on the earth, because they also don't know Me and don't love Me enough to forget their stubborn "doctrines" and lay aside their preconceived ideas and find Me for themselves. Many will love their denominations, pastors, and their own ideas much more than Me. That hurts Me so. It cuts Me like a knife because I adore these people and wish only goodness for all men.

Many pastors will not be with Me because they are teaching My People wrongly, and the things they will not teach the people are in many cases worse than what they do teach. They are afraid to lose their money, popularity, and support from their congregations. Woe unto you pastors who lead My Darling Sheep, My Beloved Children, astray. Do you realize that on the earth you represent Me to these people? You are to be fatherly overseers of the flocks of My People. I know it is not easy and you struggle. I hurt for you, too, because I love you so much. Never think that you are less important to Me than the sheep are. But your Father in Heaven beseeches you to say what I tell you to say. Wake up and draw close to Me and do not fear what I want to show you, especially "have no fear of man." For days are coming soon when it will be between you and Me anyway.

The day soon approaches in which each man will be responsible for only himself, and I will deal with each of you according to your works. It is not My Intention to make any of you afraid, for fear never really solves anything. What I want is to help all of you. Please believe Me. You are all My Creation. I love you all, to the depths of My Being. I even love the Antichrist. Yes, it's true. Because My Nature is Love, I do not differentiate between people, thinking because he is evil, I hate him. No, he is still a human being, and I love all the people who have ever been. I do not love his sin or yours, but that does not mean I hate anyone. I sent My Boy into your world to save you from death and torment. I did the only thing I could do to help you, and it was also the most painful thing for Me imaginable. Yet, I was also joyous just to be able to save your lives.

So I plead with you. Don't turn away. I want you with Me always and forever and ever, just as I created you to be. You were made for a purpose, and that was so that We could be together as a joyous family, which would begin on earth, then move into heaven with Me to have fun and glorious times forever together.

I love you so. Please believe Me. Jesus loves you and My Holy Spirit does, too. We are waiting for you. We look forward to your meeting Us and loving Us, too.

We want to be one big, happy family with you forever. Love, THE FATHER.

(John 16: 12 I have yet many things to say unto you, but ye can not bear them now.)

SECTION 1

DRAMA OF THE AGES

I t all began in a garden far away in time. Out of dusty earthiness, I formed a figure and blew into him the breath of My Own Life. I lit him with My Own Power, the light all men are lit with, for I am the Light of the World and the Light of All Men. Yet, in all his nobility, Adam was made out of dirt. I had to illustrate the fact that, though he became the "god of the earth," in that I gave him authority and power over it, yet he was still an earthen vessel and I was God of All. He would have to walk in humility, knowing this.

The first Adam, then, was eventually going to be a creator upon earth, placing his creative, life-giving seed into the secret place of the womb of woman, where it could grow to form man and then My Family—the Body of Christ.

For out of Adam, the creator, came also a child, a beautiful woman created from man, birthed out of Adam's own bone of his body. For in the marrow of bone is life produced, for there is the blood supply created, and the "Life is in the Blood." Sweet, gentle Eve, who was supposed to be protected by her strong, adoring husband, was used by the Devil as her husband watched her sin innocently. Still, "ignorance of the law" was no excuse in Satan's book, since he is the great legalist. I was ready to forgive and forget the whole thing if only the man I created had acted like a man. Instead of repenting for his wife, he immediately grabbed the fruit of the knowledge of good and evil from her and bit hard, sealing sin in that moment. Have you thought that not only did I not want My children to know about evil, but also I didn't want them to have the knowledge of good, because good was only good when compared to evil? For I only wanted them to have the knowledge that I would give them when I knew they were ready for it, and ultimately the knowledge I wanted them to possess was who I was. There was to be a learning process through their lives, and that was to know Me more and more with each day that passed. That was My Beautiful Plan. It was to be a wonder for them to have the incredible, ever-increasing joy of knowing their God in all His Glorious Love that would unfold to them as the pages of a golden scroll.

I, the "Ancient of Days," would open to them the mysteries of the beauty of My character and the excitement of the treasure of the lovely garden world I had bestowed upon them. They would never have lacked for joy. Yet in the moment Adam sealed the sin by his failure to be a man to his wife, the two died. I do not tell you this to be an accuser of Adam, but to point out what really took place so that you can avoid this in your own lives.

Adam was created to be earthy, strong, and masculine—a part of nature. Eve was created out of Adam's body, and she was less earthy, more gentle, and delicate. Adam was, so to speak, a cowboy, a lumberjack, a rancher. He was a gardener and keeper of animals, created to be brawny and powerful. Eve was to be the sweet mother of the human race, birthing out of herself children who would coo and gurgle and be pampered by their gentle mother. Adam, on the other hand, was to be a wise and strong father, just as I am. He was to be an illustration of gentle strength.

Then, an animal came into the garden more beautiful than all the rest. Think of it—he was more gorgeous than all the others that I had painted with the colors of My lavish, dramatic paintbrush. For I was not measly with My creation, but I painted earth's canvas in splashy, dashing rainbows of radiant colors, creating all manner of beauty upon the face of the earth. Consider the iridescence of the spreading plumes of the peacock or the lovely pink flamingo against a blue tropical lagoon, the icy-white snow tiger amidst dark green jungle foliage, or the flashing gleam of the blue-black panther, darting among lush jungle trees, and you will know that I have adorned your world with great wonder.

Yet the serpent was more beautiful than all these. He was

created by Myself to be a great tempter to test My creation before I would place children into their lives and before I could give them more knowledge of their God. In his beautiful sing-song voice (for you will remember Lucifer was also a musical instrument, he literally contained music in his own body), he flashed his awesome beauty provocatively, mesmerizing the woman with his loveliness just as a child is transfixed by a fiery-colored butterfly. She was captivated, captured! With melodic words, he weaved his charming spell and lured the innocent insect into his web. And the man watched as "innocence" was snared in a trap, then gleefully joined in sin, chomping on the "fruit of evil." After he did this wicked deed, Adam then pointed his finger at his wife in disgust saying, "The woman you gave me," and accused her before Myself and all of heaven, who looked on. Satan, the serpent, flew up to Me, as a sneaky tattletale, to boldly accuse My created ones of sinning against Me. He only was able to come before Me because he knew his time had not yet come when I would cast him down, down, into burning rivers of molten fire to scream in torment forever. He is still able, to this very day, to come up before Me as the cowardly "accuser of the brethren" that he is, pointing out your faults, but not forever. For I have appointed an hour for the renewal and restoring of many Adams and Eves who are now in the world.

For My children shall be brought back to their original glory on planet Earth in the end time of the age. Their feet shall be as hinds' feet in high places in mountains of spirit. They shall, as a great army, take the land once again. The men shall be restored to manly strength, while the women will once again become revered objects of love and gentleness. Man and woman shall resume their roles I cast each into—in all their glory. They shall return the earth to the Lord—My army, spoken of by the prophet Joel. Great shall be the terror of evil people and devils that are in their paths.

They shall go out in the strength of the Father as conquerors, heroes, knights in shining armor. Finally, men and women will conquer the evil that has been waged against them for so long. For they shall take the land just as their brother, Jesus, did. In the last of time, people shall be restored to who they were meant to be. You men, I would have you, even now, begin to take back from evil all that was given to you so long ago.

You married men, take back your bride I have given you. By tender mercies and love, win her again. Take back the land, the oil, and wine, the cattle on the hills that I own, which I created for you to control, not a bunch of "crooked stockbrokers on Wall Street." For these things are Mine, and they are yours because you are Mine. Take back your children, the inheritance I have given you, to bring you gladness and to fill your quivers full. For the children are to be your crown and blessing and joy. Speak it out, "Great is the peace of my children." Take back My inheritance for Me, your God; that is, the people of "My harvest of the earth."

Be strong and full of courage, knowing the Greater One lives and makes His temple, His Holy Place, His dwelling, in you. I wish to do greater marvels through you than your minds can fathom. Take back the land and earth for yourselves and Me. You ask how. Pray fervently, and I will show you great mysteries. Ask and you shall receive. Seek and you shall find. Seek My face, the face of God, that only pure spirit, not flesh, can find, and you will know the way. Ask Me to show you the open door to mysteries as yet unheard of and unseen by you, paths and ways to God. There are hidden things that you do not yet know, secrets kept until now, the end of time upon the earth. Don't delay. Do not wait. Seek Me, that I may show you things that no eye has yet seen, no ear yet heard, thoughts that no mind has yet thought, except the "Mind of Christ. Look for Me, and I will be found.

ADAM AND HIS EVE LIVED IN BLISS

Every moment was fruitful, interesting, filled with unexplainable joy. Their garden—for it truly was theirs—was so exquisite, so divinely beautiful. It was the paradise of the earth. The garden was temperature-controlled at all times. Even when it became warm, it was not an oppressive heat, but a relaxing warmth to be basked in.

The water surrounding Eden was not frigid, but tepid, and delightfully satisfying as the couple swam for hours at a time. There was a special effervescent quality about it as with a clear and cool bubbling spring that flows out from deep within. There were many exquisite fish in the waters that were their frolicking playmates. The forest floor was fresh and perfumy as they stepped upon it. Sweet, heady fragrances drifted everywhere because the garden held every imaginable lovely blossom. Exotic spices and herbs hid among the foliage and trailed their perfumes in sweet waves upon the gentle breezes that blew through Our garden. It was their perfect gift from Me. I was its creator, and they were its caretakers. Adam was a husbandman and Eve, his precious helper.

There was no jealousy or anger between the two. They were always in joy and laughter discovering new wonders, as two sweet children. My "two innocents" held one another's hands as they passed through paradise, and their giggles and songs and sweet conversation could be heard. I created a pure and perfect love between them. Yet, they possessed their own minds and wills. They could roam freely in their lovely home.

And then you know the story; the serpent entered Eden. He was so gloriously beautiful. They gasped when they beheld him, for they had never laid eyes upon an animal that was as gorgeous. Alas, he offered them a bite of pride, and they bit. What was sweet as honey in their mouths became bitter as gall.

The two who had been fed a perfect diet of sweet juicy
fruits, aromatic herbs and succulent vegetables had bodies
without an inch of unneeded fat. They were physically fit
and had the perfect amount of muscle, beautifully toned.
Adam's golden body rippled with sleek muscles, as one of
the deer he loved to frolic with; Eve's body was softer, yet
was smooth and taut. When they ran, they resembled the
beauty of gazelles darting and leaping effortlessly upon
high peaks.

When My two beauties slept, My Father's heart was
touched by their sweetness, as if seeing two white doves
cooing in surrender. I watched them always. When they
awoke, they drank from the cool cistern in the garden and
ran giggling to grab pomegranates, slurping as the ripe
fruit juices ran down their chins, then to the date tree to eat
of the chewy, sugary fruit. Another day of wonder thus
began in beautiful Eden.

But, alas, when the fruit of disobedience was fully conceived, they ran from My arms to hide from their Daddy.
Suddenly, I threatened them. I was a fearful object. They
had not known fear of Me before. They had loved Me, so
they had nothing to fear. But now, I was not the close, loving Father, but their judge. Yet I longed to forgive. But, as
always happens with sin, people judge themselves. So on
that fateful day, they left their gentle home for the hellish-
ness of the "law of sin and death." They had been so blessed
and left so cursed. The world outside was not temperate; it
was a desert inferno. There were wild animals, earthquakes,
and not enough food. But what was worse than all this was
that they left Me. I could no longer protect them as I had
because they were now sinful. There was a gulf, a curtain of
sin, between them and Myself. Now, Adam often sulked as
he sweated while eking out a living. He became irritable
with the one whom he had adored. His thoughts were sometimes of other women, and Eve was hurt because she wanted the one whom she had been a part of. They were

separate now. When they were joined in sex, they felt a oneness, but when not, they sometimes quarreled and felt
unfulfilled. Life was different now. When Eve bore her own
fruit, it was in writhing pain. They now saw the ugliness of
blood and excrement and smelled bad odors. The animals,
which had been their playmates, were now their enemies.
Only their fires at night kept the animals from devouring
the family. And so the two became many peoples and
tongues. And man was snared in the seduction of the serpent ... trapped. You know the rest. I sent My Son to be the
sacrifice, to pull man back to Myself and to Eden. I was
able to at least rescue some of My creation. And now I look
from the Garden to the end of the age, the span of cen-
turies, and I long for the family I started so long ago, all of
Adam's and Eve's brothers and sisters, all tribes and peoples of earth. I longed to set things right between the man,
his wife, their children, and all of you. When the two
walked out of Eden and away from Me, they walked into the
waiting arms of the enemy who would almost devour them.
The wonder and horror of it was not something I ever
wanted My darlings to know. For they were My babies, and
just as you have babies and want to protect them, so did I.
It was a horror to watch as they roamed the earth experiencing all the dreadful things I never wanted for them. The
two lovebirds became wounded cock-fighters sometimes
devouring one another even with their tongues, just as you
now do. Yet through all the years, I still kept them, and
there was still some beauty even in the desert of their existence.

Now that the end is near for all of you, I wish to restore
man to the beauty of fellowship that we once had. I want to
return him to Eden, to the glory of really knowing Me
again. For you see, I am Eden. I am paradise.

I long to help you escape the wicked world. I long for
you to come into a relationship with Me and with your family that is exquisite. You may not be able to return to Eden

or paradise at this moment, but there are places in the spirit with Me that are bliss and joy forevermore. Look away unto Me, the author and finisher of your faith. Look away unto Paradise.

I CREATED A DIVINE ORDER ...

for man's well-being and wholeness. Man was made in My image and was to live in beauty and freedom and orderliness. But when Adam and Eve fell from grace, things changed from order to chaos. There was still an element of order to their lives, but the perfect balance they once had was gone. By their disobedience, they set wheels creaking into motion; wheels in the Spirit Realm that should never have been started. When Eve was deceived, it was a terrible thing, but when Adam sinned knowingly, it was much worse. It was compounded by the fact that immediately, Adam blamed his beautiful Eve, whom he adored. The gentle, adorable creature I had given him, the sweet child, Eve, was suddenly a scorned object. In that horrible moment, man hated the One who loved him, and a process began. Innocence died and evil stalked in its place. The eyes of the two lovely children of the garden opened as if awakened from peaceful, blissful sleep, and they saw each other as if for the first time, stark and naked. They felt disgust, rejection, and fear at what they perceived to be the nakedness of the reality of their bodies and of their humanness. Suddenly, theirs was not the gentleness of the quiet, tranquil garden where peace, beauty, and laughter were their sweet companions. Now, the sleepers had awakened to the harsh realities that would greet them with every new turn. For they had been two beauties, asleep to all that was unlovely or painful. Theirs was the dance of lovely swans locked in sweet embrace, in a world gorgeous beyond human words.

Now the loud clanging of an alarm clock went off in the

realm of spirit. Time to arise and greet the hungry Devil. My heart broke to see My creation fall away from Me. I longed to forgive and forget, but they wouldn't let Me. Further and deeper into sin, they fell away from Me, each new step taking My children further from My Father's heart and into the claws of the evil one; alas, out of the warmth of the garden to live in a cold and harsh world. I saw it all, and My heart broke. My children of the light became dark. I saw the years ahead and the future generations down through all of history and I felt the pain of it all. Had I not been "The Creator of All," I would have died from the agony of what sin would do to My creation for the ages to come. But then, a little light twinkled; a tiny light pricked the blackness, a thought, a whisper of a thought. There might just be a way, a Human who would feel pain, just like My children, Adam and Eve, and all their children; a Man who would come from the womb of a woman, screaming with the pain of life as He was born just like other men. A Man who would be tired when He awoke, but would have to get up and work like other men. A Man who would get thirsty and hungry and would be tempted as all men are, but who would overcome all things because of My great love for mankind. It would hurt this Savior Man and Me, too, because He would be separated from Me as if ripped away from the One He was a part of. But in the end, the pain of it all would have a great purpose—to buy back what was lost from Me, My created little ones. At last, gruesome, evil creatures would have no right to escort them into the belly of Hell, but now angels could stand ready to usher them into paradise with Me. Paradise that was lost, now could be found. Now, at last, man had a chance for beauty again in his life. And I could rest knowing that I could have a family with Me forever.

To you who are alive in the earth today, I say, I know your trials and your plights. I know that things are not perfect, that you are living in trying and terrible times. But it could have been much worse if I had not sent the Son to your rescue.

I know the days grow dark. I know the fiery trials that overtake you at times. I also know the "way out," the escape. There are times in which these trials are a war waged against you in the Spirit Realm, by the enemy of your souls. There are times, too, when I must allow you to suffer a little while for your own good so that you can learn lessons and be strengthened. But believe this—I never do anything to harm you. My motives are for your good only. I long to see you win the skirmishes and wars of your lives. I long to rescue you even from yourselves. I am the God of peace and righteousness and I long to crown you with joy, even in the midst of a riotous world. I long for your souls to find rest, yes, even in the lion's den. You say, "This is not possible," but I say it is. For I can shut the mouth of the beast and make him a kitten. In the eye of the whirlwind there is a quiet, unearthly peace. In the howling winds and rain of a storm, there are dry caves for shelter. Even in the earth, there is comfort. Am I not mightier than earth? Did I not make the earth? Am I not strong enough to protect My children from all that is ahead of you and all that you are experiencing?

In the days ahead, I will give you new weapons of the Spirit that will help you also in the natural realms. Music and praise will become mightier and different than they have been. Where you have had stones and slings, I will give you nuclear weaponry. Just have hope. Be of good cheer. Lift up your heads, that the King of Glory can come into you children. I know your thoughts. You think in your hearts, if things are this bad now and the birthing pains have not really begun, how will I stand what is coming upon planet Earth? I say, My children, little ones, you won't stand. You are too weak; but I say this day that One who is not weak will stand in you, dear ones. I will carry you through the flood ahead just as I carried Noah upon many deep and deadly waters, just as I carried Job and David and all those who cried out to Me to save them from deep waters. I shall carry you, too. You are small and light, and I am as strong as the ages, the universe, and more. I am able and mighty, and the enemy is as a gnat to Me. Even the feared Antichrist is as a pesky fly to Me that I will one day flick with My finger into the bowels of Hell with all his host, never to be bothered again by them. For now, they are only instruments for My purposes, but soon they will be cast into torment forever, never to bother My family again.

Fear not, little flock, for it is My good pleasure to give you keys, keys to open up places you have never been before in the kingdom. There shall be new keys and they shall be weapons to win against the evil one. For I love you, My children of the light. I said I would never leave you or forsake you and I meant it! You will never be alone; I have sentries always watching you, guarding you. You are top priority for Me. When you are in danger, the red alert sounds and I come to your rescue; the Commander-in-Chief leaps into battle, and the puny enemy flees. You are safe, even when you feel you will drown. Didn't I say I'd make a way where there seemed to be no way? Ponder that when there seems to be no way, when the situation literally seems impossible; then is when I will change the impossible to the possible. All I ask is that you mind Me and do your best. I know you'll fail at times. I am not an Egyptian taskmaster, but I do ask you to try. That way, the enemy has no legal right to you because of disobedience. Also, try to love, really love, each other. You are not perfect yet. You each have faults. You are, after all, just people—flesh and blood. Try to give each other sympathy because of human failings and human misery. You may try to cover up your feelings, but you all have your share of pain. Try to see good in your brothers and sisters.

You will need each other in the days ahead. I am able to change even the worst faults and turn them into the most beautiful elements of man's character. Again, dear sweet ones, you have your Father's love, admiration, and respect. That may sound strange, but it's true. Even though I created you and you fell, I still feel good things towards you. My thoughts towards you are filtered through the blood of My Son. They are pure thoughts of love and joy when I contemplate my dear children. I love you all. I love each of you. I love you, My child. I am with you and in you, even until the end of the age.

CRUCIFIXION!

Even the word summons thoughts of terror and remorse. There is an evil and gruesomeness about it that makes words fail. When little children first hear stories about crucifixion or their parent explains what the word means, the child can hardly believe his ears. "You mean they actually nail someone to a cross, Mommy?" the child asks in utter disbelief. "How can that be? Why would anyone do that to another person?" "It doesn't make sense, does it, sweetheart, but that is exactly what evil men sometimes do to people," Mother replies.

The crucifixion of any human being is almost too terrible to contemplate. Yet when My Son, The Lamb, was slaughtered on the Hill of Skulls, the horror of it shook creation. Golgotha, that lonely hill where so much blood had been spilled, now would "catch and drink up the Pure Blood of the Man" who would save all men. For His Blood was the very Blood, the very Life of God The Father. You see, He carried to earth a part of Yahweh, the "I AM" with Him. He also brought down into the lowliest of the low, the Spirit of Holiness, the Holy Spirit. For on that awesome day that the Savior's foot touched the earth, God also touched it.

After almost dying from the cruel sweating of blood in Gethsemane, He knew in His heart the worst was yet to come. The pressure of the decision He had to make nearly

took His life there in that lonely garden. He wrestled with
His flesh all the long night and with Me. He knew My will
for Him and yet it had to become His will, too. He had to
embrace His own suffering death or the sacrifice would not
have been perfect. All through the lonely hours, minutes,
and seconds of that dark, gloomy night, He lamented, tor-
mented, questioned, wept, and pleaded with Me to remove
"the cup of gall" that He would have to drink. All through
that dark eventide, I had to watch My Son suffer like no
other man ever had or would, even to the sweating of blood.
Other humans have sweated blood, but never for the reason
My Son did. He had a foreknowledge of what His death
would hold for Him. And I knew it would be even worse
than He could know then. When the daylight broke and His
joy should have been to see the beauty of the rising sun, yet
there was only a bit of relief from the bitter night. The decision to do the will of the One who had sent Him to earth
was made. He finally "gave up" and gave His consent to perish for mankind.

He was then almost immediately taken before evil men
who belittled Him, men who tried to intellectualize who He
was and His mission. Those men did everything they could
to break His spirit. They looked at Him with amused con-
tempt. He held fast, however, because He knew the final
glory … men's very lives.

Then He was taken to a street and made to carry upon
His tender back the instrument of His death, His cross, so
that you would not be forced to carry the spirit of death
around in yourself. He was then stripped of His clothing,
made naked, so that you would not be stripped of your dignity and your covering, the Holy Spirit. His worldly goods
were stripped away so that yours would not be. He was spit
upon and mocked and His Kingship removed so that you
could be a king and a priest. A crown of thorns was roughly
shoved upon His head and the nail-like thorns even pierced
His skull and eyes so that yours would not be pierced and

so that you could be a king. By now, His mind was dulled by shock so that your minds could be clear and

you could have the "mind of Christ." He was whipped with glass and sharp metal objects attached to the flailing, cruel bullwhip, and His internal organs were exposed so that yours would not be. Those stripes, those slick-raw cuts that opened His flesh to the bone were done so that you would not have to experience illness. Each one of those whipped stripes represented a major illness; the number of them coincides with the number of major illnesses there are in medicine. This is why He took the horrible lashing, so that you might be healed and spared in yours and your children's bodies from sickness.

Then His torn, ripped body was thrown onto the tree that He had dragged to the place of His imminent death. Splinters penetrated His broken, sweet body and then, horror of horrors, long spikes were pounded fiercely into His gentle, loving, merciful hands. Those hands that had touched so many with the greatest kindness the people had ever known, those sweet and vulnerable hands, were now being pounded and nailed to a tree. Then His feet, which had run to help those in need, were broken as the nails crushed His bones, for I say, "How lovely are the feet of them who bring good news." This was all done so that your ministry could not be stopped. He was then hoisted into an upright position where He labored, gasping and lifting His ribcage with every breath, so that your breath would not be stopped. The sins of mankind were then heaped onto His Body, Spirit, and Mind. This was the greatest atrocity of all, for in that moment, all the filthy menstrual rags of sinful man fell like outer darkness onto one man, THE BEST OF ALL MEN. The stench that He smelled was beyond all smells imaginable, for sin has a smell. He absorbed sin, so that you would not have to. He even, worst of all, "became sin!" Then His own Father had to turn away from His Son. Jesus was now alone so that you would not have to endure loneliness and be alone without a family. He was then offered a drink of sour vinegar, the "wrath of God," so that you and your babies would not have to taste of it.

Finally, His poor Heart broke for you. The temple veil tore, because the Heart of God broke in the Spirit, broke for the love of man all that day, also. But as the veil broke, God was revealed to man. On that day, the precious, gentle Heart of Jesus, the Father and the Spirit, broke for the love of man, for all men who had ever been and who would ever be, because of love.

The pain that mankind caused by doing wrong killed Jesus and, in killing Jesus, killed a part of God and the Spirit. On the day of Jesus' birth in that lonely stable, with only a few animals around Him, the Father also came to earth and humbled Himself to man. He, in essence, bowed to His creation and allowed Himself to be born into the bloody womb of a mortal woman and to live, suffer, and die for that woman and all people everywhere. When Jesus died, God's heart broke for His creation, for He and the Father and Spirit were one.

The sacrifice was perfect and unflawed, or it would not have worked. Sinful mankind had to be rescued, and there was only one who could do it: "the Grand Hero, the Good Captain of Love," the One who was sent down to waiting, delicate, weak man to save him from himself.

The devils had danced in glee before Jesus came because they thought they were the winners. But "the Captain of the Sky," "the great rescuer," had other plans and He prevailed; He won and He shall truly reign forever and ever.

The King has won and sits upon His throne and upon many waters, and He truly does rule the nations and men's hearts. He did it all for you. He won the great battle at Calvary for you because love made a way for you!

THE GREATEST LIE OF ALL

The most sinister lie ever perpetrated on man has been the lie of man's unworthiness.

When the first sin was committed, the serpent convinced Eve that God did not want her to have all knowledge; that somehow she was inferior and was not loved enough by God for her to know good and evil. She believed him. She then hurt the human race along with Adam. However innocently, she still gave away her glorious birthright, as well as that of all people's, because of a lie. When her son, Cain, killed his brother, Abel, again it was a feeling of unworthiness that made Cain jealous and afraid of his brother's perfect sacrifice and ultimate favor with God. And again, when Job mourned and bewailed the fate that had beset him, his unworthy feelings led him into the sin of self-pity and blaming God.

When Mary sat at Jesus' feet, Martha became indignant and jealous because Mary wouldn't work as Martha did. Unworthy feelings kept Martha from being at Jesus' feet. Underlying all sin is a sense of unworthiness and inferiority. Children first learn it from parents who don't love without stipulation, parents who won't love freely without any reservation. Children grow up believing that if the ones who created them can't love and accept them, then how could anyone else love them, even themselves. This lack of self-love and self-acceptance can work on a person inwardly and not appear to be the reason behind so many, many problems, even sin. If I feel I'm no good, then why not go out and sin to prove how "no good" I am? I will sin and fail because I am unworthy to succeed.

What has been the ultimate purpose of Satan in using this deception, in putting this on people? Satan is supremely intelligent. Why would he choose this seemingly not-too-important tactic? Because it can undermine every single aspect of a person's life. It is a strong, strong delusion, an ultimate weapon, like a nuclear bomb. He can make man, through his own feelings about who he is and how he thinks God sees him, suspicious even of God's motives and then not love God. The goal he has is to separate God and man. Many have gone down the path to hell through this deceit.

It goes like this: I feel badly about who I am. I hurt others because of it, then they hurt me. Then I really feel badly about other people, and worse, about myself. Round and round it goes, and then at the end of the cycle, I really don't like God and He must not like me.

These things can be so subtle. They can be so hidden, way back in the places of the mind. They can be the cause of all sin: murder, envyings, strife, etc. This can be the clincher, the frosting on the cake, Satan closing the deal and you've bought the product: the big lie!

What does God say? He says, "I'm not like anyone you've ever met. You cannot even begin to imagine My nature or character or My feelings toward you. They are so good, so very, very good. I meditate on My sweet thoughts towards you. Do you hear? I meditate, dwell on, deliberate, think about, ponder, talk about, discuss, even shout about My lovely feelings toward you. You are My treasure."

When a mother and father bring their long-awaited baby home from the hospital, it's their most precious possession. They'd kill or die for their baby. They are in love with their child; they dote on the blink of its eyes or a little yawn. They watch the baby when it sleeps and is awake, when it eats, plays, and oh, the joy when it talks and walks. The baby becomes their world. They would lose all they owned to preserve their child. So it is with Me, but so much more. I loved you enough to give My perfect Son; He and I were One. I loved you enough to give Myself because He is Me and I am Him, and I love each one of you as much as My Baby, Jesus. He was My Boy, My Child, My Sweet Baby, yet I love you just the same.

Know you have suffered enough from the feelings that have haunted and torn your soul for so long. You never had to carry them. These feelings have ruined relationships with others and in your own life, too and have sought to ruin even Our relationship. Ask Me for a new way of seeing yourself and a new way of seeing Me.

Let Me help you. Ask Me to help you overcome the evil one, who would use this lie above every other lie to destroy your life. It's time to fight him!! It's time to be angry with him and get him out of your life! He's eaten away silently as the cankerworm too long, and you have been unaware and have not fought him enough through deliverance prayers to Me.

Let him who has stolen steal no more from you. I am the way to life.

THE VAGABOND

The spirit of the vagabond is the spirit at work in people who are referred to as bums, derelicts, lowlifes, or vagrants. These are all cruel names for a truly "cruel condition." The vagabond is, in a word, an outcast. In certain parts of the world, especially Middle Eastern countries, when a crime is committed that doesn't require death, the perpetrator is, many times, cast out. He is sent away from his home, family, town, and sometimes even his country. He is then considered dead to his family and friends. Even his name is not to be spoken by them. In many ways, death would be kinder. Many people in Eastern countries work under their parents and relatives in family businesses. When a person is cast out, he is then unemployed, and it can be difficult to find work elsewhere. Then poverty sets in. In your country, there are an increasing number of street people. These poor unfortunates, much of the time, end up involved in drugs, alcohol abuse, and tobacco. These vices oftentimes accompany poverty. So it is that the spirit that is over homeless people is that of the "Curse of the Vagabond."

This curse is an ancient one. It began with Adam and Eve—my two lovelies who inhabited paradise, fell from grace, and had to be cast out of their heavenly home, Eden. They became drifters, wanderers for a time. As if being cast into a wild and dangerous land wasn't bad enough, they had two sons who would break their hearts. Cain would eventually kill Abel, his brother. Cain was a type and shadow of Satan, while Abel was a type and shadow of Jesus. Cain's sacrifice was a blemished lamb, which was unacceptable. When his brother Abel gave a perfect sacrifice to Me, Cain murdered him. He then was cast away from his family, but not without being marked. The mark was a warning from Me that no man should hurt him. In a day, Adam and his wife Eve lost their two children forever. They had entered through the door of sin, and they were to find many of sin's children waiting for them in the new realm into which they had ventured. For the "father of sin" has many offspring, none of which you want to meet.

Poverty is one of the most terrible of all sin's children and this one almost always accompanies the curse of the vagabond. Poverty is like a tree with many branches and deep roots. Poverty kills people, literally! Nations are starving in your world today. Along with starvation come diseases of a magnitude that are gruesome indeed and are soon to become horribly, unbelievably escalated in your world. Mind-dizzying diseases are about to be loosed upon planet Earth as a direct result of the very thing that brought on the "curse of the vagabond," that is, the sin of man.

The prodigal son was one of life's victims of this terrible curse. He was a victim in the sense that he had let Satan dupe him into leaving his safe, secure home with his kingly father. Actually, more than just a parable, this story is really an analogy of what happens when a person sins.

For when he sins, he leaves the protection of God's umbrella and ventures into a hostile and unknown realm.

The prodigal son lived in paradise with his father, the king. He was a prince, and as such, was entitled to live in and possess all the glory of the kingdom with his dad. Things in his life were good, yet an evil spirit entered into him and made him want to sin. A spirit of discontentedness will often cause people to fall. The prodigal son had been living in bliss for a long time when he had the thought occur to him, "Why not try just one little night of fun." After that first night, more and more followed, until he was totally snared by the devil and his cohorts, the demons. Now he was a prisoner of sin. Ultimately, in utter despair, he was reduced to "pigdom," eating out of troughs. He shared slop right alongside filthy, stinking pigs. He ate rotting garbage because he was that desperate. He drank filthy water and slept in manure. He was little more than an animal now himself. Sex, parties, and drink had been his friends, but now he had sunk into an even lower lifestyle: that of the derelict, the vagabond. Now he was marked with that evil spirit, and many of its children moved in. Poverty, uncleanness, sexual immorality, and on and on the list continued. He was the picture of a filthy, broken man. He was cloaked in sin. The pigs he dined with were really a type and shadow of people in the world who have sunken into the depths of depraved humanity. He was, now, the lowest of the low. He was a street rat, a vagabond. He had thought sin would be fun, but sin is only fun for a season. Then the wages of it take hold and with ugly claws, death grabs its victim. Now the prodigal son was a helpless prisoner. He had nowhere to go and no one to help him. He was alone in the world, an outcast. Yet as he struggled in the depths of despair, someone was watching him. It was I, his God. For I had never left or forsaken him. With a tender heart, full of love and compassion, I watched and waited for My child to come home to Me. And then the blessed day arrived. I caught sight of My boy coming slowly up the path. He was still a long ways away. My heart leapt. Tears of joy streamed down My cheeks. I arose quickly from where I sat and began to run to him, first slowly, then wildly in sweet abandon. My beloved was closer now. He saw Me, then stopped, and hung his head. I ran faster. Then he was in My arms, safe, secure. "I love you, My precious son," I cried. He began to sob as I held him tight. "I'll never ever let you go again," I whispered. We walked home arm in arm. Our joy was indescribable. Then I placed a jeweled crown upon his dirty, matted hair and laid the finest robe upon his crusted shoulders. Upon his bare and bleeding feet, I slipped on golden slippers. He begged Me to let him bathe first because he was so dirty, but I couldn't see the dirt. I could only see My beloved child, the love of My life. I bade him, "Sit by Me, son." We then had a party and celebrated My darling's return. Now he was restored to Me, now I could help him to heal from the world's filth and sin. Glory flooded our hearts and even the servants in My castle rejoiced for us. Life was now complete.

This is how I long to restore and revive My little ones. Whenever there is sin, it takes you away from Me. The thief truly wants to steal you away from your Father. Just as the prodigal son fell under the heavy spell of the "Curse of the Vagabond," many of you have fallen under sin's curses. Many have come from families that were steeped in sin and then poverty followed. If there was only one curse that ever came upon people as a punishment for sin, it would be poverty. For when a person sins, his own heart judges itself, and poverty is usually the method. He feels so badly about himself, so worthless and insecure and that he is unworthy of riches. Money is one of the ways in which I bless people. It can give people much joy and fun in life. Like an overjoyed child who is given a new toy, so it is with you. It is nothing to be ashamed of. I made you like this. I created the world and things in it for you to enjoy. The Garden was

Paradise. Everything in it was wondrous. "That is truly what all of you desire." You really want Eden. You want heaven. Next to My Spirit, prosperity is the next best thing. I say to you, "Put off the spirit of sin, which brings all manner of curses, and put on My Spirit, for I wish above all things that you might prosper first of all, secondly, that you would be in good health, and lastly, that your soul, your mind, would prosper and be overflowing with joy."

WHY DO YOU SUPPOSE I USED THE ILLUSTRATION OF A BOAT ...

and water to explain about faith when Jesus and his disciples were in the storm at sea? It could be said that they were on the sea of life with all its troubles, in a lifeboat with Jesus. The disciples, however, did not really know how close Jesus was to their situation. He was actually a part of it! He was there. He was involved and He was concerned, but because He was a human being, He slept. However, His Spirit was not sleeping. Just like you, His Spirit never slept. The one part of a person that is always on the alert is the spirit. Even in sleep, the spirit is always thinking and observing.

When the winds of life began to blow and howl across that great sea, then the waves started to toss. The once calm, gentle ocean suddenly had whitecaps. The waves were now furious. Because it was a somewhat small wooden boat, just as you are small, the disciples knew it could only hold together for so long. You also feel that way—that you can only keep it together for so long. The boat was starting to take on water. They knew they were in great danger and drowning was imminent. Isn't that like all My children? In danger, you forget how close Jesus is to you. You are even more blessed than His disciples because now, He is living not just with you, but He is now inside of your very bodies, minds, and spirits. As they saw what looked to them like a hurricane. They pictured in their minds what drowning would be like. Don't you sometimes see visions of what it would be like to drown in life's troubles? Doesn't Satan sometimes serve you "a feast of fear" over your present or past situations or even the future? When the waters of tribulation churn and boil in your life, don't you feel tempted to doubt ME and that I am with you? The disciples were just as human as you even though the Master was in the boat, their boat, their situation. He seemed to be removed by sleep ... gone. Finally, He awoke, and they cried out, just as you do, "Help us, save us! Many waters are trying to drown us! The waves would pull us under and suffocate us as we sink to the black depths!" It was a moment of truth! Their lives had not been in such danger since they had been with Jesus. It was one thing to deal with other desperate people: the sick, the insane, those who were terrified that their own babies and loved ones would die or continue to be sick, but when it comes home to self, that's a different story.

This is the spirit of Job's friends. Hear Me again, this is the state of My church! When the other guy is suffering, My church might pray a little for that person, but when it comes to doing something sacrificial, like giving a large sum of money or taking up the plow and helping a brother work, they are reluctant and usually unwilling to help. The Amish are a wonderful example to Christians everywhere. When a brother's barn burns, the community rebuilds. What would have taken one person weeks and left his animals outside to suffer, with many people working, only requires a day. Besides, good deeds always, always come back to a person in blessings. It may not be in the same way, but you always get back what you sow, whether good or bad. With faith, you will get back the good, multiplied.

When Jesus saw the waves and winds and that the enemy sought to kill not only His disciples, but also Jesus, He commanded, "Peace, be still," and they obeyed. The disciples were not the ones Satan sought so much to kill, but he wanted Jesus. He remembered back to the garden when he was told there was coming One who would "bruise the head of the serpent." He wanted the Master. But Jesus only had to speak a word and the nuisance of "a gnat," Satan, was rebuked. Then Jesus did a strange thing. He beckoned Peter to join Him and come out and walk upon the waters. He was, in essence, saying, "Peter, you now can walk upon the mountain of troubles I have conquered for you. It is under your feet as well as under My blood, because I am on top of this situation, literally, in My body. I am physically walking on and have overcome this mountain in your life, Peter, and you and I are standing upon what would have destroyed you had I not taken over and stopped it. But I did stop it, Peter. You and My friends here in the boat did not go down into the deep, into the depths of Shoel, but you lived and, I hope, learned a valuable lesson: that I am with you always, even until the end of the age." In the days ahead, you will all have many opportunities to be tried by fire and water. Never fear, daughter, Job's friends will also be tried by fiery trials if they are to become gold. Those who are having "not too hard a time" will shortly come to understand what you are experiencing. In their hour of need, I don't want you or yours to say, "I told you so," but to help them in kindness and humility, just as I do for you. I never say, "I told you so." I just help you. When the mountain of water looms so high you cannot even see the top, say to it, "Peace, be still, be cast into the sea" I mean this literally. Say this to the mountain of troubles, "Peace, be still, you will be cast into the sea." Know that it must obey your words, for they are My words, spoken by ME coming up through your spirit, into your mind and out of your body or mouth. Those words echo from the deep places in you, from your Tabernacle, your Holy of Holies, your inner spirit. They then come up to your soulish realm, your mind, and finally find residence in the member of your body, your tongue, to then be loosed into creativity, just as I created earth with My words. This is how evil is bound—by your words. It is the principle of binding and loosing. Don't be afraid you cannot do this. I don't expect you to do the miracle. That's My job. Only believe when you say it, that I am big enough and faithful enough and that I care enough to change evil situations in your life. Most of you act like you think I don't care enough to help you. That destroys your faith and then you have to live with the painful situation. Don't you realize, I care more than you do about your life. I am a daddy. I watch you adoringly as a father watches his small child. But I care more than an earthly mother or father. Most parents love their children so much, they would truly want to die if their child did. I love you more than that. I did die, some, when My Son did. It was more painful to see Him tortured by My created humans and take all sin upon His gentle, kind body and then be thrust into the torment of Hell, than if I had died Myself.

But I did it for you, My created ones, My babies. If it was necessary, I'd do it every day for all eternity for you. But it isn't! It only had to be done once. It was complete. I love man so much. Without ME, you are as helpless as a newborn baby. Believe Me when I say I am here to help. Enable Me to help you. I long to. My heart aches to help you. Command, yes, demand the works of My hands. Get emotional; cry out to Me! Then I will hear from heaven and heal you and your situation, your land, the mountain that stands in the way of the fields that you would plant in your land to bring forth a good harvest.

Say this prayer:

Evil situations in my life, Jesus speaks through me to you, "Peace, be still." You will bow to the Master Jesus. You will cease by the power and glory of the Holy One to have any more control over me or mine. You and all your workers of iniquity are cast into dry places as far away from me and mine as the East is from the West. As you leave, you will bow your knee to Jesus and say, "He is Lord." Now where my life and all mine who I pray for have had our lives swept clean of evil situations, come then Holy Spirit, and fill us and our lives to the overflow with the goodness of God. Cause us to prosper in all the areas of our lives. Cause us to taste your banquet of heavenly fruits in our lives. Bless us with an ever-present, everlasting blessing. Amen.

DID YOU EVER FEEL LIKE YOU WERE SURROUNDED BY ENEMIES ... ?

Whether they are your spouse, family, children, friends, co-workers, classmates, or acquaintances? It is a horrid, sad, just plain awful feeling. Believe Me, I do understand! I was surrounded by enemies in My short-lived life on your planet. Even those who were supposed to love, support, and understand Me, didn't. And then there were those who were absolutely pitted against Me. They feared and hated Me with a vengeance. I could have "taken them out" with a breath, a word, a thought. But I couldn't, because I had created them. They also were to be instruments used in My Plan. How the crowds loved Me and then how quickly they turned. It was sheer pain to be accused, hated, and rejected by the "ones whom I had created." I do understand what it feels like to be betrayed by My Children. So if your children betray you in the days ahead, remember that I endured it, too! Remember also that they are under strong delusions. For the "spirit of hypnosis" or "the trance" will hold many of these children captive. Just as Hitler's youth, they will become captives of "Egyptian, mesmerizing spirits." Some, however, will wake up and come to their senses. My Overcomers—My "Army of Zion," My "Sons of God," My "Swat Team," will be the instrument that will be used to save a lost and dying generation.

You may feel that you are living in an industrial garbage dump, and you are. The green and glorious garden earth that I created has become "Pollution City Dump." New and horrid chemicals are being produced in your earth in droves each day. My Beautiful Earth and My Beautiful

Creation, how I weep for you. For those of you who live in big, teeming, dirty cities, I "feel for you." I know what you endure. PLEASE know this. I am informed, up-to-date, cognizant of, aware of, watching, looking, and listening always, every nanosecond of every minute to you!

I am in the earth. I am there in My overcomers, My intercessors, My prophets, My people. I am Resident in their spirits. I, the Godhead, do bodily dwell in My Children. Then, My Holy Spirit is in them and in the world. He roves about watching, listening, ministering in the compassion of My Spirit. Then, too, I have hosts, bands, troops of angels as many as all the sands of the shores, ready and at My command, surrounding, protecting, and waging great heavenly wars for you! Heaven's host is strong and well armored to fight the evil ones for you. For the host of heavenly "battle-savvy" warriors are skilled in the fight. Know this—they are, and I am, strong and mighty in War!

You may look at other people and think, "They look so happy, and I am so sad." My trials are just horrid, but know this—that other person may not be as anointed as you. Besides, they may be a good actor. So do not despair because you see others who have it so much better than you. There is one thing that trials do—they give a person "battle savvy."

I will say this, however, and that is that many of My People suffer some things in life needlessly because they either lack faith or are deceived in an area. They need My Knowledge poured out upon them to defeat the enemy in their lives. If you're sick, ask for knowledge and then wisdom to know what to do with it. This goes for areas of poverty, problems with children, etc. Some of you are so religious with your kids that they want to spew, and so do I. It is a shame, because instead of drawing them to a loving God, you do just the opposite. Religious man, filled with legalism and hellfire and damnation preaching, has lost more people for Me than have all other deterrents to people becoming one of My Flock. There is a fine line, a narrow walking path, that leads to the salvation of yourself and others. When a parent becomes overzealous—lecturing, belittling, hounding, sermonizing their children—-they are in danger of losing their babies' eternal souls as well as their own soul. This is not the method for winning anyone to Me!

What if, every time you sinned, I appeared to you in a vision and explained your sin, how it hurt Me, how you could correct it, etc.? It would definitely be a deterrent to sin, but it would be harassment. When My prodigal, way-ward son (you) left Me, did I seek him out and then proceed to do all the above? Did I lecture him about "the next time when he came home to Me?" No, I ran to him in sweet, lov-ing, excited abandon. I was thrilled just to be in his pres-ence, just to be close to My Precious! Some of you parents have problems that you refuse to deal with—-past hurts and marriage and relationship troubles. Some of you have so buried all the pain that it just seeps and spills! It washes over onto your darlings or even to other people. Then I look like "the Bad Guy" to them! Again, "I don't care for Myself," but I care for them. My creation doesn't need to have a bad view of the only One who truly can help them—their Friend.

Now I must speak about a subject that is a real problem to people, especially kids. It is out-of-marriage sex. They are being sold a "bill of goods" that it's okay, especially if the two are in love or "consenting adults." I must tell you; it isn't okay. I made sex to be first, a spiritual sacrament, an act begun in spirit. There is also a legal aspect to it, that the two have made covenant before becoming one in body. It is part of the shedding of blood. It is part of My Crucifixion, the Blood Covenant. It is as binding as death. It is the covenant that My Son and I made when He shed His Blood for all sin. It is the same blood-binding covenant that two people make when they marry. Without the virginity of the woman, however, there can be no shedding of blood. What does this signify then? It signifies that two virgins join together to become one—just as the Father and Son did (in Spirit and in Body—although not sexually). The two people are then "one flesh." It is mysterious and deeply fraught with much meaning. Sex is a deep mystery and not one that I wanted shared out of wedlock. For the Blood Covenant is sacred and personal. It is not something to be shared with anyone but your mate. What if Jesus had gone "whoring after flesh?" Read the Word. He went to taverns and spent time with the sinners. He drank wine, but never abused it. What if He had decided to get drunk and have sex with a woman? What if He had lied to Himself and thought, "I made that woman over there. She's My Creation. So what if I want to have 'a taste' of what I made?" What would have happened then? I will tell you!

The Perfect, Unblemished, Sacrificial Lamb would have become spotted with sin. It would have had to have been cast into the fire, leaving no sacrifice for you. You may say, "So what?" But I say this. "You can thank your God every day that My Son was a gentleman, never taking advantage of any woman." Because of His obedience to Me, you live and so do your children and families! For if My Precious Child had not been perfectly obedient to the Cross, you would be in Hell, you and yours.

So the next time you want to have illicit sex, read what My Word says about it and how it can keep you out of My Kingdom! I am not trying to punish you by keeping you pure, but I am, rather, trying to protect you.

All that I've said does not mean, however, that I want you to hound your children about not having sex. You can discuss it in many ways, on many occasions, if they will listen, but hounding them will make them rebellious and could even drive them to it. Treat this subject with great wisdom, for they live in a tempting world, and it will take wisdom to overcome Satan in his battle to get your children.

There are trillions of things I could say to you, but I will leave My Spirit to talk to you and gently minister to you.

I have prayer warriors covering you each day! I want only goodness and mercy for each man! I love you so very, very much that My Heart would break for the love of you ... except that I AM GOD!

I wish you all every good thing being poured into your lives' cups. I wish for your cup to truly run over with the goodness of the wine of My Spirit and of your lives. I ADORE YOU!!!

I AM WRITING ESPECIALLY TO PASTORS ...

and those in ministry. You know, I never want to insult man. I say in My Word that I am not offended, and I never am, for to be offended is to be small, narrow, and actually arrogant. Offense says, "I am not worthy of another's criticism, scolding, or even a well-meant statement that touched a sore spot." I know these things can hurt and then can cause man to react badly. I do understand how you feel. I do know how sensitive you humans are to pain inflicted by other people. Just ask Me to help you with this, because if you become too sensitive about your feelings, you can actually draw painful situations to yourself. This definitely holds true in other areas of life, too. Haven't you noticed that when you are weak or wounded in an area of yourself, you will keep getting beaten up in that area? This is explained in My scripture where I say that when a person lacks, "what little they have will be taken from them." This is a principle that Satan loves. Consider what happens to a soldier in the heat of battle who's shot in the leg. The enemy sees his weakness and moves in for the kill. What happens when you are in deep financial trouble? Every time you turn around, bill collectors are contacting you. Then, your landlord calls or comes by, demanding his rent, and on and on—things snowball. Satan sees weaknesses in you and uses them to his advantage to try to overcome you and your family. You see, others are adversely affected by your problems, too. The answer to your being offended or being overcome in areas of your life is Me. Pray to Me to develop a "tough skin" about yourself and to not be overcome or stolen from by the enemy of your souls.

So then, ministers, please hear Me, please, please hear what I want to tell you (and please don't take offense). I tell you these things in love. Things must change! I must tell you this, whether you heed the words written by the prophet or Me or not, your life and your church are shortly going to change, drastically!

Think of yourself literally as a shepherd of a flock of sheep. What are the duties of the shepherd? First, a shepherd feeds the sheep. He must lead them to lush pastures where there are plenty of meadow grasses for them to eat. Then the shepherd has to find pure water for his thirsty flock. The good shepherd then takes the sheep to a place of safety where they can rest and sleep. This is a particularly important phase of being a shepherd because the sheep are the most vulnerable at night. Out in the night, lurking wolves and wild dogs can lay in wait for their chance to move in for the kill. They definitely know when the flock is the most open to attack. There are other times when the sheep are susceptible, namely when the shepherd goes out to hunt for even one lost sheep and during lambing (the birthing of the baby sheep). All these duties of a sheepherder are your duties, too, men and women of God. I give you milk to feed the infant sheep, the young in the congregation, and "strong meat" for the older Christian sheep. The more mature the child of God is, the stronger and heavier the mysteries of God that he can contain. Actually, in this area, many pastors don't correctly evaluate their congregations. Many of the sheep are much more mature and hungry than you shepherds realize. Of course, there is a difference between idle curiosity and true hunger. If a person is truly hungry, he will eat and digest what he has been fed and then use the wisdom and knowledge for good purposes for himself and others. This is explained in My Word where I talk about the seed falling onto fertile ground. The fertile ground is the hungry heart. The hungrier a person is, the more desperate he or she becomes. Many, many of My sheep and also your sheep are desperate. They are living in very, very desperate times. I want you to hear Me say this to you. The sheep may come to church on Sunday morning looking polished and perky, but inside, they are anything but that. They are "good actors." They are really in the worst trouble they have ever been in in all their lives. For night is fast upon these sheep and out in the dark lurk hungry wolves. Their mouths are dripping saliva as they watch the naïve sheep settling down for a comfortable sleep. In the quiet and peace of twilight, little do the sheep know that the wolves are checking out their "next meal." Who are the wolves? They are the henchmen of Satan, his evil workers of iniquity—his dark servants. They are the "tares," or weeds, who rub shoulders with the sheep (the wheat) in the pews of your church. They are not "true seekers," they are "true users." They are in your church because they want to gain something for themselves. They really don't want Me and they don't want to help you build your church up in godliness; they are curiosity seekers trying "to get wisdom and knowledge, but not for pure purposes." They want to lavish the deep knowledge of God upon themselves for their own selfish purposes. Then, too, they are in church to look good to others. They wear "sheep suits" and they portray sheep very well, indeed, unless a person has good discernment. Shortly, however, all the alluring, tantalizing temptations that are shortly to pour upon planet Earth will be too much for them and they will go over to the "other side." Do not mourn for them, for they will be right where they belong. You may be surprised when you see who they are, though, because they look so wheat-like, so good! Many of them have posed as Christian believers for a very long time.

The main point I want to make is this. The sheep are in "big trouble." They are at the mercy of the wolves and they need protection, and not just on Sunday morning or in a Wednesday night prayer service. It's not enough! When My Son, Jesus, went out "on the road" with His disciples, He lived among His sheep. He was close to many of them. Maybe that isn't as practical in your day and age. There are so many people now on your earth. However, I can tell you this, as the overseers of your churches, you and your disciples (teams of ministry) need to get closer than you ever have been to the flock!

Here is the essence of what I want to tell you. There have got to be drastic, drastic changes in your church, not in a year from now, but now! Whether you choose to go My Way and begin quickly to implement these changes is up to you, but you will suffer great loss if you choose your own way! For I will have obedient shepherds who will tend My sheep.

Do you remember when you were children? I called many of you to be shepherds then. Perhaps you pretended to preach to great throngs of people. Perhaps I spoke to you and told you you'd become shepherds, or maybe you just desired it! However you came to be a minister of Mine, you obviously had a desire to help people and share Me with them. At first, you were excited, anointed. But then, the fire in your hearts burned more dimly until now, many of you have almost lost your flame. Without the anointing from Me, the whole "church business" is a very ritualistic and boring one.

Well, I am here to give you another chance, but it will require courage. It is true that revival is coming and that is a "great hope" to all of you. However, before an incredible dinner, there are hors d'oeuvres. As with most wonderful events, there is a prelude. What does a symphony orchestra do before a concert? They "warm up." Well, it's "WARM-UP TIME!!" Here is the first step of the "revival hors d'oeuvres" that I want you to do. I want you first to forget your reputation, just as My Son made Himself of "no reputation." Do you think there were not lots of people who said negative, hateful, gossipy things about "My Boy?" The Pharisees, the great (so they thought) religious leaders of their time, pompously twittered among themselves about My precious Son behind His back. They were, of course, unaware that someone was listening, namely Me. I didn't like it! They sarcastically asked each other, "Who does He think He is?" I, of course, knew who "He was," just as I know who you are. The Pharisees were eventually dealt with just as your tormentors will be, for I do not take lightly those who interfere with the workings of My Spirit. So pay them no mind, those who would speak evil of you. In essence, I want you to become radical! Your church boards will come around if you are strong and don't back down. Remember, you are the leader, not them.

Secondly, I want you to totally change your services—everything! Praying, ministering, music, teaching, preaching, prophesying. I want to use the prophet in a new and glorious way. People in the congregation need their questions answered for theirs and their families' lives. As confusion and desperation permeate your world and people's lives more and more with each day that passes, your sheep will become frantic, and I do mean frantic! You don't want them to secretly go to psychics (who are not of Me). You will want them to go to the prophets. I tell you this, "Prophecy is the ministry: the order of the day!" It will become the most enlightened, glorious, incredible, anointed ministry that has ever been on the face of the earth! The prophets will do such marvels, such wonders, that they will defy description. Because of the glorious new wine that will be poured out through the prophets ... I tell you this ... Satan hates them! Because of this, they are and have always been number "one" on his hit list. He uses all sorts of deceptive devices to destroy and ultimately annihilate them. If he can get the church to do this, even better. I tell the church very, very solemnly to be careful! Touch not My anointed! They may not be perfect. They are human and do make mistakes, but they are allowed mistakes just like any other ministry. That is why I created schools of prophets, so that they could grow into their ministries. You shepherds have been given the greatest gift in your prophets. Use their ministries mightily, greatly!

Everything must change! How do you do this? You ask Me to show you. Soon, your congregations will be taught personally by Me, for doesn't My Word say that you have no need of man to teach you? However, for now, I will allow teaching and preaching, but it must be timely. Many, many of you ministers don't seem to really comprehend the times you are in. Strong troubles in people's lives call for strong measures. You and your sheep are standing on the brink of the edge of eternity. You are looking into the abyss and yet over it looms the heavens and eternity. Many of your sheep will surely fall into the pitfalls of what is shortly to be upon them and you unless they have a strong, strong shepherd. They don't just need a strong shepherd, but they need strong helpers, too. There are a lot of sheep out there in the flock, and the shepherd needs strong teams of people to help them. During the revival on Azusa Street, things changed, namely the world! There was no preaching or teaching unless a person in the congregation was led to give a word. There was no formal music program. Everything was directed and orchestrated by Me. No fancy collection plates were passed. Only simple boxes attached to the wall held the tithes and offerings. The church totally trusted Me to handle the finances. Only when man "stepped in" and tried to regiment things, did the glorious revival "fizzle." That is what I am trying to tell you. Take your hands off "the wheel" and let Me take over. Have you ever heard a person give testimony about how he was headed for an auto accident and he took his hands off the wheel and the car came safely to a halt? There was no accident because I took over. That's what I want of you, too—just let go of your church and your service. LET GO ! Let Me have total control. The first step, hear Me, the first step, minister, is to BE QUIET. The sheep are well able to pray and cry out to Me. They are well able to minister to one another, too. They know more than you think. There are all kinds of ministries sitting among the pews (among the ewes—a little joke, but true)! There are fabulous end-day ministries ready to be birthed at My beckoning in your church. The greatest thing you can do as a father figure is to bring them out into the forefront and into the five-fold ministry.

Next, know this: there must be a sacrifice just like in the Blood Covenant before I can move. Any time I have ever moved, there was someone ready to sacrifice himself, someone who would not only die to himself, but more importantly, "come alive to Me." Lazarus had to die so that he could live again. This person must give up his "own way." He must become in tune with Me. He must intercede in prayer over his church so that many can live. For I tell you this, Mary Magdalene is sitting in your church and many more Marys are just about to "come in." Because she was a loose woman and I saved her for Me and from herself, she is now extremely grateful. I tell you this, the new Marys (whether male or female—for there is neither with Me) are going to be even more grateful because they will be literally "pulled out" of "Pits of Sin" and into My Kingdom. I tell you this solemnly, "you won't be able to control them," for they will truly be "awash, ablaze" with gratitude and with My Spirit; not that you will want to control them, for they will help to usher in the revival.

Next, I want you to bring in people who can teach finances, not like much of the teaching that has been before, but teachers with VISION, supernatural teachers who will tell the sheep how to become kings of the earth instead of the servants of the evil world-system. There may be those in your congregation who are financial apostles, too. If so, use them to help the sheep sidestep the horrendous poverty that is coming upon planet Earth. Also, My sheep desperately need emotional as well as physical and ultimately spirit healing. New ministries of a never-before-seen magnitude are even now being raised up to fight the enemy and minister in a supernatural glory to My lambs.

Most importantly, though, when the sheep begin to see the coming miracles, they will become more and more excited!

Now, here's the clincher, pastor. I want you to get a team of people who can be in your church all day long and even all night long for the needs of the people. These "ministers," these intercessors and prophets, will be there to fast, pray, intercede, and especially prophesy in rooms with the sheep for the purpose of intercessory prayer—praying for the saints. These teams with healing in their wings (hands) are to minister to the little ones who come to them. They are to offer up strong prayers for the saints and not waste time in any kind of idleness. They are to be creative and dedicated ministry teams, waiting for all manner of people to come in to be ministered to.

If you do these things, shepherd, your church will explode in a glory that you cannot imagine! Step out and do the "greater works" that your big brother, Jesus, did! Remember, you ministers are also sheep—My sheep. Surely you would desire that I minister to you, too! So give up "your way" and your church's "antiquated way" of doing things and tap into the spirit of the "here and now." For truly, I say, life must change, and change is at the door!

I love you so, dear one, and I greatly, greatly desire to bless you and I will, if you will obey Me!

SECTION 2

DEAR ONE, I LONG TO SHARE MYSELF WITH MAN

Mankind has known so little about Me. I have created man for Myself—for Me. It is My grandest gesture—creation. In the darkness of the universe, I was lonely. I wanted to love and be loved, and so I created a man in My own image and likeness. How can I convey to you how much I loved man—you? If you have a child or someone you love, think of the feelings you have for that person. If he's your child, think of the pride and tender feelings you have for him, then multiply them times two trillion and you will have the beginnings of My love for you. I love you so!!! I feel love towards you with such a range of feelings. I am drunk and faint with love—as My Word says. I have an almost overwhelming love for you, for My creation. I long with cords of longing to touch My child...to touch your depths with My Spirit. I long to stir you—to show you who I am.

When My Son hung on the cross for you, it was horror beyond human imagination—but it was also because of a passion for man. Because love was what controlled and created the cross, there was dignity and sacrifice in the face of naked cruelty. My Son, so like a soft, baby-white lamb, so sweet, hung by nails that you might live and not hang by nails and so also that your babies might not hang on crosses.

Oh, that you could just have a taste of My love revealed to you. That you could understand that all My actions towards you are measured and directed by love.

If you saw your child lying lifeless and white with death and knew you could never speak to that little one on this earth again, how would you feel? Your sorrow would reach to the heavens. Do you know when you turn away from Me that My heart breaks, too; that I have feelings like you, but because of My vastness and ability to feel, I feel the pain so much more acutely than you?

Even when My children turn away from Me and are unhappy, I feel this kind of pain. Man is coming to a place of not being able to hear My Words as easily as in the past. The earth is on a downward spiral, and when tumultuous days come, man will not have the opportunity to clearly hear My Words as in this writing.

Perk up your ears; awaken, My love; listen for My voice, "for the winds of time are blowing." Oh, that you'd know and care that I love you so. I love you endlessly, timelessly, completely. I am not like some television soap star. I don't love you, then leave. I am not like an abandoning husband.

I love you as a tireless, dedicated, compassionate, gentle husband loves his wife. I would never hurt you. I would only build you up into a godly person, a completed creation that I can admire and then say, "Well done."

There are so many things I long to share with you, deep things that you wouldn't be able to understand yet.

The message of the hour is "to know Me, now." Who am I? How do I think? How do I act in a situation? Why do I do the things I do? Do you know Me? If not, let Me show you who I am.

Pray that your joy may be full. Fast and wait for Me to come to you. Sit quietly and let Me show you just who "I AM."

I AM THAT ... I AM.

FORGIVENESS

To all who are alive upon your earth, I salute you! For just to survive in your dangerous world is tricky at times. Of course, I desire much more than for you to just be a survivor—my highest desire is that you be an "overcomer." In order to overcome the evils of your world, it is imperative that you learn to forgive, totally and fully.

So many—in fact, most people in your world—are

plagued by unforgiveness. Why is this so? It is partly because of pride. This pride says, "How dare you hurt me or mine." I tell you this, it is pure foolishness to assume that you will not get hurt living on your planet no matter how good or kind you are. For you live in the "war zone" of the universe. As I watch and listen to the sights and sounds upon your soiled world, I almost shudder. I hear the clamor of war. I see the carnage of death, too, and I tell you this, this is not the natural, normal fighting war between nations. No, this is a much more insidious war: that of the battle between human beings. This clatter of war is being fought in offices, in courtrooms (especially divorce and child-custody courtrooms), in sporting events, everywhere, but most of all, in the homes of families. Children, especially teenagers, are at war with the parents who created them and desperately want the best for them. Husbands and wives battle one another for control. I do not say this to hurt men, but once again I must tell you that the Adamic spirit is very much alive and well. This is the spirit of man that did so much damage. This Adamic spirit did incredible, absolute, horror-of-horror damage and destruction to the human race, but then as a sideline, turned on the one whom he had betrayed and betrayed her once again to Me. This gossipy, self-righteous, totally selfish spirit "winked" as it tattled on Eve, exclaiming, "The woman YOU gave me!" This evil, deceitful, sneaky Adam-spirit even accused his Creator of giving him someone who was flawed, blemished, inferior, a second-class person. There were in this statement even undertones that I, his God, had not only failed him, but even tricked him with a tarnished gift. Actually, Eve and I were both "the accused." But Adam knew better. He knew his sin, because his heart condemned him as he ran to pick leaves to hide his naked shame! How many of you men still run to hide from Me (the One who loves you)? You still point at women with hatred seeping from your own wounded hearts. Women are still your scapegoats, Adam. Who really truly suffers in your world? I'll tell you who: your victims, Adam, first women, then even children, sometimes your own. I tell you this. They are not your enemy. For the Eve woman that I gave to Adam in answer to his desire for a mate was so totally sweet and gorgeous. However, she just wasn't good enough for him. Adam knew how evil he truly was, though. For at the betraying moment, his once-kind, gentle, and wise heart cracked like stony granite, and it's been cracking ever since.

Quite frankly, men are the ones who find it the hardest to forgive because they are the most arrogant. The "how dare they" syndrome is still so very alive and well. How could anyone hurt Adam? I have news for Adam: he was the one doing the hurting. Billions of babies have died because of Adam. Women suffer so many varied assaults from him that human words fail Me. The world is in chaos because the Adam-spirit is behind every corner of man's heart. Women sin, too, but much of their sin is in answer to Adam's sneaky hatred.

Please, men, don't think that because a woman writes these words that she dreamt them up to punish you. She is a pen and I Am the author and finisher of your faith. You may think I am picking on you, but I am not. I just want you to get straightened out so that I can have one big, happy, earthen family. I don't wish to condemn, but only to restore. I love you so truly, so completely, I never want to inflict wounds upon any of you. Please, please believe this.

Other people are not your problem or enemy—Satan, the Dragon, is. When you refuse to forgive another, you tie and chain yourself to that situation and the person you hate. I know some of you have lost children to violent, evil men. I know how it claws, strangles, suffocates you, because I lost My Boy to My very own creation. Consider this, you have never watched with your own eyes as cruel, jesting, brawny, muscled men spiked your child to a tree (like the donkey in the game "pin the tail on the donkey"). You, worst of all, never had to turn away from your precious because He was too "lousy with sin." You didn't watch your darling's flesh melt and rot and fill up with the "dragon worms" that only a total filling up of sin brings. You didn't have to watch "shark-creature-demons" zip in and yank His Spirit into the open grave of the earth that led to the "burning ember worms" in Hell. Your last look at your baby was not seeing "those eyes" that cried out through raw, gushing carnage, "I love you, Daddy, and because I love you and all the little ones You and I created, I'll never ever, ever see You again. Tell the angels good-bye, Daddy! Tell all heaven good-bye. But remember this, My precious flesh of My flesh, Father, now you can have all Your babies back with You. I do this thing for them and for You ... precious God, My Father!"

And with that He was gone! Count yourself lucky that you didn't have to watch each of yours die like that, because I tell you this: the cross-death was to be theirs, your babies, if My Son and I had not interrupted and inter-cepted man. You may say that you haven't committed sins bad enough to send anyone to Hell, especially My Son, but I say, son, daughter, you single-handedly sent the Lamb to Hell. Your seemingly insignificant little mistakes were enough to "nail Him."

So, the next time you are given a dirty look or someone says something that cuts you or whether you are raped or someone you love is murdered by another, remember, Son of Man, My Words. At least you didn't have to pay for all the seamy, rotten, stinking, parasitic sins of the whole of humanity with your beloved child's life-force blood. You didn't have to watch the gushing, spilling, then drop after drop of blood fall to the earth as your precious "bled out" His life for an ungrateful, unloving, foolish-beyond-belief race of humanity. Be glad you were never asked or made to pay the ultimate price for mankind's sin ... that is, the tor-ture, death, and walk through Hell's portals that We paid for the love of you. When people hurt each other, they usually do it by ignorance. They don't generally sit around dreaming up schemes to hurt you. People are sheep in the truest sense of the Word. They are sheepish and walk in foolishness almost beyond belief. They absolutely, positively "know not what they do." They are darkened in their understanding. The worse the sin and the sinner, the worse the darkness. Mankind is truly worse than animals. Animals don't torture and maim; they at least are smart enough to kill to eat. Man is the vengeful one. Man, unlike animals, hates. Animals do have emotions, but they do not hate just for the sake of hating. If their offspring is killed by another animal, they might take the life of that animal, but they would not sit around seething in anger. Animals, in that respect, are kinder than men.

So the next time you need to forgive someone, remember that a great price was exacted for their sin. You may not be able to forgive in a day, but you can at least "choose to forgive" in a moment. You can make the decision to forgive. You may not feel anything (no flashing lights or bells going off). You may not feel very much at all, but don't be deceived when you make that decision. We in the Spirit Realm see a great process beginning—that of the cutting of "hatred ties." You, in essence, do one of the most profound things that a human can: you set yourself and the other person or people free. In that act, you allow them to go on to hopefully become a much better human being, or if they will not repent, you allow Me to work on them. I always try to work in love, but if that fails, then "vengeance is Mine, says the Lord."

When a person will not forgive (release another), then the tormentors come to torment him. How horridly sad, because the offense in itself already caused pain.

Know this—your vengeance will not truly ease your pain. I am the only One who can take away pain. I am the "analgesic." I am the painkiller. So many of you suffer needlessly from poverty and illnesses because you hate. It is buried deep in your souls. You need a washing in the depths of your heart. Ask Me! I will never let you down. Ask me to take away the "victim spirit" from you and the one you need to forgive. The ultimate good is the restoration of you and the one who needs your forgiveness. All heaven rejoices when you forgive because then you are lifted up to God and you walk in your high places.

FOR MANY OF YOU, YOUR ENTRANCE ...

into this cold world may have been highlighted with glaring lights and a stinging slap on your precious little bottom. Then after this indignity, you were stuck with needles, even on the heel of your tiny foot. Some of you were removed from your mother and behind closed doors were subjected to tests that were not pleasant. True, some of them were for your own good, but nevertheless, they punctuated your not-so-glorious birth into the world. Then there were vaccinations and trips to the doctor and the dentist. There was that first day of school, too, which was horrifying for many of you, and perhaps the succeeding days and years in school were very uncomfortable and scary for many of you.

Perhaps friends betrayed you or teachers judged you to be bad or hopeless. All these things are the normal occurrences of American life. But when you add, perhaps, family problems, possibly with yelling, screaming, and violence, then you enter a whole other realm. God forbid that you ever had to endure sexual abuse or, worst of all, Satanic ritual abuse, but many people have. Many children are sexually abused by friends and family as well as by strangers these days.

When you entered the realm of earth, you came to a wild and evil place. As if the natural traumas weren't enough, the unnatural evil acts done against innocent children are the breakers of hearts and the causes of all manner of fear, chronic anxiety, depression, and diseases of the mind. In one way, I am so very saddened to see anyone have to go through the "veil of tears" that is your world. I see it all, every little hurt, every horrific wounding done against people. My heart breaks from it all because I am so much more sensitive than any of you. I see it all clearly from heaven, and though I am God, there are times I even blush and wonder at the horror of what people do to one another. Man's heart truly knows no limits to evil. The Bible says "the heart is unbelievably evil, who can know it?" Only I can, because it is limitless in its capacity for doing despicable deeds. Then when Satan enters into the human heart or situation, a multiplied power comes into play. When you add the intellect of Satan to any situation, you have trouble. How I long to cradle and shelter you from life's troubles. How I desire to change bad situations in your lives. As the world grows darker, you will need Me more and more.

All the troubles you will suffer in life are why I say to rejoice at a death and mourn at a birth. However, life is not impossible. I did not dump you into the earth and then just leave you there, a helpless victim. I do give humans certain survival skills. But for My chosen ones, I long to equip you with nuclear weapons. I long to bring back the years that were eaten by the worms and locust. So much has been stolen from you. If you really knew the extent of it, you would be overcome with sorrow. This is because you live in the world with the great "thief." He loves to steal families, finances, friends, health, jobs, fun, joy, happiness—the list goes on and on. But I am "The Blesser." I love to give. I love to bestow all goodness upon My beloved ones.

Know this deep inside you, that I am here to help you. There are no earthly words to tell you how I long to help you. The only way I can say it is "that I come out of Myself to help you." Part of Me left heaven to help you through Jesus, My Son. Then, My spirit is with you always, hovering over you and through you, helping your failings. You are covered, even though most of the time you are unaware of it. However, when you sin, especially habitually, that is when you become uncovered. Then, "my umbrella of safety" leaves you for a time, because when you sin, you enter Satan's realm. That's why it's important to fight against sin in your life. Please, get serious with your sin and with your past. Get things cleaned up quickly. Be willing to do anything it takes to get the past healed in your life, because it still controls you! This is the hour I have ordained to heal My people, but you must be willing to do it any way I choose. I am The Great Physician. I am the healer of your soul.

Remember, little darling one, I am gentle and kind and full to the brim with tender mercies. I want to see joy upon your sweet face much more than do you. I truly, truly love, admire, and respect you. You are a gentle fawn to Me, and I see the beauty in your kind eyes. I am so sorry your heart has been broken in two, but I can also mend and bind up the brokenhearted. I pour My gentle, fragrant, perfumed oil into the cracks of your soul and you are gloriously healed. I am the great sealer of your heart and mind and the healer and health of your sweet body. I truly love you, My little precious one.

HAVE YOU EVER WONDERED ...

why so many people are so sad? There are so many, many unhappy, sorrowful people on your earth. This unhappiness and dissatisfaction actually has its roots in childhood. When a baby is born into the world, it is brand new. Her sweet little body is covered in new flesh, pink and smooth. Her little bones are tiny, strong, and pure white. Her eyes are sparkling bright. This little baby is a brand-new little human being, so full of promise. This is why people are always smiling and so taken with a newborn baby. But there is more to it than that. What people are actually seeing is the creative hand of God at work. My creation is the greatest thing I have ever done, for it included My Son, Jesus, and the cross! Creation is the basis for all things, because without My creation, nothing exists except Myself. In creating, I formed that sweet little baby. Just look at a little infant someday and meditate on the incredulous workings of its little body and how everything works so perfectly. See how the joints move, how the eyes blink, and know that you are beholding a miracle of God.

But, sadly, little bodies do grow up and become injured and scarred from just being in your world. Constantly, you are being besieged by toxins of all kinds. The aging effects of the sun are always with you. Your food, water, and air are impure, for even your planet has aged. Just like that baby, your world was once new and fresh. The air was pure; the water sparkled with clean effervescence; the soil was rich and clean. Everything on your earth was life giving and sustaining. Beautiful, healthy fish jumped joyously out of rivers as bears lumbered down to the creek's edge for cool sips of water. Cats flopped down in the noonday sun to have delicious naps. Antelopes sniffed the living air and danced away into the forests. All was well and beautiful on your planet.

What joy there was just in living and drinking in another breath of sweet, fresh air. There was a rhythm and mystery to life. There was such glorious, glorious beauty in the creativity of a brand new earth. And, of course, the loveliness of the dewy-fresh garden, Eden, was beyond compare. It was a magical place of joy and undiscovered mysteries. In fact, Adam and his bride, Eve's, great joy was to explore "paradise." It was supernatural. So, then, My beautiful children were placed in a garden by the hand of the Creator just as a tiny seed is placed into the garden of its mother's womb, and in both, there was and is the glory of creation. When that child leaves the protection of the Eden-like womb, it enters a dark place—earth. All manner of terrible things can happen to that little human, and as the years go by, the growing child begins to see the light. The child starts to see the world, not as the place of promise that it once seemed to be. Now, the child has scars. Many are on the inside. For those children who are abused, the scarring can be horrific. But these woundings and scars are invisible to most people because they're hidden. Then there comes a day when this child wakes up from his sweet sleep of childhood and realizes he isn't living in Eden; and his heart breaks. For those children, this new revelation can be shattering. Like a pretty glass falling to the floor and breaking into a hundred pieces, so, too, these little hearts break from their freefalling into "life's abyss." Then, hope is gone and their lives can really seem to be over. Though their physical bodies live, their minds and spirits shrink from so much sorrow. Your earth is full of people like this. They become machine-like because they are literally broken inside. Do not ever think that terrible abuse and sorrow cannot break the mind and spirit, because it can. The bones will even dry out from a broken spirit. Yes, there are even physical repercussions to this terrible breaking. But then, picture all those broken pieces of glass zipping up, supernaturally, onto the shelf from where they were knocked over and see them coming back together, perfectly. That is what restoration is like. Restoration is taking that wounded child and making him the sweet, brand new, perfect, little baby he once was, but 'even better. Now he is even stronger than he once was as a baby. Restoration is not just restoring what was lost, but it is adding to it. Wasn't Job given twice as much as he had? Job was the richest man in the world to begin with. Just think of the wealth he was given. After his affliction, he was then blessed with more children, animals, lands, happy years of life, and even more. He lived in a beautiful wilderness area, which was his Eden. For after his trials, he came out shining like gold.

So, too, with you. I desire, want, long for, have a purpose

in My God's Heart-of-Hearts that you be restored. For listen to Me, hear My words, "It is only in this restoration process that you can be healed wholly, made rich, delivered out of the dirty, bustling, crazy, cities in which you live, and be given the power to overcome all manner of evil in your lives and in your earth." Because you have traveled so far from Eden, you have got to be brought back by the hand of God. There is still a form of Eden in your world. Does My Word say I destroyed it? No. It says that I placed angels on each side of its entrance, but not that I destroyed it. Only in a protected place will you be able to survive the coming holocaust. My Word is full of directions to paradise. I say to go down by the sheep gate, go by the tent cords, go out and sleep on a bed of cedar branches, etc. to go where the flock is drinking from the waters. I talk about the deer panting for the water-brook. These are all a picture of My people being called into their Eden, their "Promised Land." This is a real place of serene beauty, a place under the doorpost with My Son's blood washing and spilling over it. There is splendor there. You will not be sick or age in this place because these things are part of the sin-system of your world. In fact, I must tell you this—you will have your youth restored in this place. Do you think this impossible? It absolutely is not! If the worldly scientists are on the verge of restoring youth to people, why do you think it strange that I, Jehovah, can do this and more? I always do much more than the world can do. Remember, I don't just restore, I add to. Do not despair, for you are about to gaze upon the wonders of heaven coming to earth for My chosen seed. FOR THERE IS A PLACE CALLED EDEN IN THE HEART OF YOUR EARTH AND IT BECKONS AND CALLS TO THE DEEP IN YOU FOR GREAT WONDER AND PLEASURE! EDEN CALLS YOU. EDEN CALLS!!

HELL'S FIRES ARE ABLAZE

They are popping and crackling with anticipation for what is shortly at hand. The demons are frenzied like angry wasps. They are insane with what is about to happen in your world. They have pet names they use to refer to each other and to your world. They like to call your earth "Den of Cush, Sodom, the cursed place, the fallen place, valley of the damned," and even refer to your world as "the New World Order." You see, they are much more aware of what is about to transpire on your planet than you are. They are, frankly, more attuned spiritually than most of you. That is not an insult to you, but it is a sad testament to the truth.

You see, they are in Hell. They are in the place of the damned. They have no distractions of pleasures as you do. Their only pleasure is to torment and torture people and the other dark spirits. So, then, even their pleasure has spiritual undertones. In other words, they are in continual spiritual activity and it is, of course, evil.

You, on the other hand, have many distractions, many things in your life that take you away from Me. Business is one of these aspects. Most people separate their job or business from Me. This should never, ever be. If there is an area of life that you desperately need Me in, it is in the matters of finance. This area of your life is very tricky for you to deal with. You may ponder and try to figure out what the stock market will do, but you don't really know. It could crash tomorrow. The only One who knows that is I. I control the raging waves of the sea and I also control great financial institutions in your earth. I lift men up and give them power, and I put them down and render them weak and powerless. Do you know what money really is? It is power! It gives men the power to buy the goods and services they need in their everyday lives. But there is another aspect to this power, and that is this, "He who controls the wealth, controls men and men's hearts." Think of the most wonder-

ful saint you know. Has this person ever gone to the government for some form of aid? You can almost bet he has.
Government aid is so prevalent and far-reaching that most
people in your country have used it. How does this glorify
Me? I am not saying that it is sin to get help from your government, but it is one of the lower, not higher, things. What
I mean is, on the "scale of glory and glorifying God," it's
way down low. You might say, "But I had no choice. My
child needed surgery or she would have died." Of course I
did not want your child to die, but that doesn't mean there
wasn't a better way. The highest thing on the scale of glory
would have been that I would have supernaturally and
miraculously healed your child. It would have brought Me
the most glory to have, in a moment, totally set her free.
Think of the ramifications of this. Can you imagine the look
on the doctors' and nurses' faces as your little girl got up
out of bed, totally healed and well, shining with My "glory-
light?" Can you see the parents running into her room to see
their child laughing and entertaining the hospital staff
with her story of how an angel entered her room, touched
her little shoulder, and told her Jesus loved her and was
going to make her well? Would there be a dry eye? And, as
the staff saw the glory-light on the child, great revival
could break out, reaching far and wide. The next best thing
would be a gradual healing, and then the next best would
be that the parents of such a child could hire the best pri-
vate doctors, specialists in their field, to care for their
daughter. But lastly, the least best thing would be to have
to go to your government to beg them for help. No matter
how you look at it, you are doing just that, begging. For "the
borrower is truly the slave of the lender." You may say, "But
it's all free." That, however, is not true. Nothing, except the
gifts I give, is free. You see, only a slave has to go to ask or
beg from someone or some institution. In other words,
there is an element of slavery involved in desperate
beseeching. Maybe the parents of the sick child didn't go

into a government building and cry and wail, but there was desperation and certainly one person, namely the government official, having power over the poor unfortunates. You see, a slave is a person over whom another human has power and control.

Perhaps there was no display of control when the parents went to the government. Possibly the worker felt sorry for their plight and sympathized with them but, nevertheless, there was "a power element at work." For every time desperate people go for help from their rulers, their rulers gain strength. The government, so to speak, "adds a notch in its belt," because somewhere, even down the road, there will be more restrictions and rules that put people into deeper and deeper bondage. Taxes will have to be raised more and more to aid increasing numbers of people. However, if the masses weren't helped by the government, there would be anarchy. Do you think if the masses were allowed to go hungry that there would not be uprisings? Looting, raping, and murder would then be "the menu of the day." This is, actually, what is in the near future. As food becomes increasingly harder to raise from soon-to-be unprecedented water shortages, people in your country will begin to die at alarming rates. Add new crop diseases and pests, horrible natural disasters, and you have the makings of a hideous end-day scenario. Then, when you put the future satanic rituals and Antichrist into this terrible pot and stir "the caldron of affliction," you truly have "Hell on earth." So this is why I say to you, "Do not let the evil world system take you captive. For this wicked, wicked system's children are all the above-mentioned horrors; and you, as children of light, should have no part in any of this slavery. I would not tell you all this and leave you with no way out. For I Am the truth and the way."

My chosen ones have lived in Egypt too long. My other children had to be removed, even bodily, from Egypt. So shall it be with you.

The slaves of Egypt, "My called and chosen ones," were delivered by an anointed man. One righteous man was used to deliver a nation. This time, because you are in a different dispensation, it will be My Spirit that delivers you. Without My help, you are as helpless as "a rock on the ground. In Me, you do live and move and have your being." Fierce days are ahead. How I wish I could spare My children. But, alas, you will go through much of what is ahead. Many will escape, but only through death or by being overcomers or by being under the protection of the overcomers. It will not be pleasant for some of those who die, but the moment they leave their bodies they'll be with Me, if they are Mine.

Now I want to talk to you more about the outpouring of wealth upon My people. I do this for two reasons: to bless My faithful ones and to help the world. This flood of prosperity that will soon completely overtake My people is going to be such an unimaginable flood that even if you tried to flee it, it would overtake you. I am sure that makes most of you very happy. You will think the Fourth of July and your birthday have fallen on the same day. You will rejoice greatly with almost overwhelming joy because it will be My joy. I take no pride or pleasure in seeing the grinding poverty of many of My own. It is a "loathsome curse" that too many of you have not been able to escape. Ministries do deliverance for sicknesses and all kinds of other curses, but not enough for poverty. Poverty stalks your world unrelentlessly and its children are hunger, disease, mental illness, broken marriages, families, and on and on. I tell you a secret thing now, listen, hear Me. Poverty is Satan's favorite curse because it is the most all-encompassing and powerful curse he can use against you. That is because poverty is a package deal. Did you hear? Just like a vacation package plan, poverty is a package plan. It has lots and lots of other amenities. It has children, and they are children you do not want to give birth to. Besides its children, it has lots of relatives. Poverty will always come down through genealogical lines. It loves to reproduce. If you could see into the spirit, you would see the dark entities pretending to give birth to other dark forces. They are begetting, begetting and propagating poverty.

Do you know what the spirit of poverty looks like? He takes the form of a bent-over old man, a beggar, filthy, and smelling so foul, so unbelievably horrendous, that if you smelled him, the toxic vapors could kill you. This corrupt and hideous-looking creature has gross, dirty, torn rags that hang off his skeletal body. This spirit has a walking stick that he constantly clutches and steadies himself with in his weakened condition. His hair hangs in dirty, gray shreds, matted and stuck to the pathetic gaunt face. The skin all over the body is scarred and pocked with large open sores, for sickness has been visited upon this poverty spirit, too. Grease, urine, and feces are smeared all over him. His pockets on his robe are turned inside out because he's "broke" and on his stick, he carries a filthy rag sack. He opens it and out crawl scorpions and stinging insects. Inside are more filthy rags, but these are bloody. These are the rags that wiped up his own blood, his victims', their children's, and families' blood and the blood of other people he's brought along with him, those he's helped to get into poverty.

You must put on your battle clothes and make war against this horrible tormentor. Satan, the "father of poverty," has a favorite "spirit-son" and this is him. He loves to affectionately call him "grinding, lack, desperation, sorrow, poor boy, not enough, never enough, sneak-thief, bad-thief, vagabond, bum." These are some of his pet names. And do you know, Christian saint, that he calls you these names, too, behind your back? He and his hordes get in back of you and bend over like the old-man spirit and tease and torment you, then fall over laughing hideously. I only tell you this to make you mad enough to get even with them. You do this through Me. You cast out this mean, twisted, bloodsucking-spirit every day ... do you hear? In fact, every hour of the day, say this, "Spirit of poverty, the Lord God rebukes you, loose you away and cast you out into dry places and bind you in Jesus' name by the blood of the Lamb, Jesus." Do this hourly at first and you will see things change in your and your families' lives. Sons, men, husbands, fathers, you are the head of your households. Act like it!

You men can actually save your families. This is your job, not your wife's. For too long, women have had to be the heads of their families. They've had to stand, but I want you men to. Do this and watch what happens. For the glory of the Father is in the latter house.

PROSTITUTION

I am writing to all those who have been in or are in prostitution. But I am also writing to tell others about this sad condition. It may not seem sad to those who are in this sordid profession, but the end of it, just as with other sins, ends in sorrow.

First of all, I want anyone who is caught in the web of prostitution or any related activities, such as pornography (porn stars), strippers, or any other sexual activities or addictions, or even murderers and serial killers, to know that I do not hate you. I do not judge you even if the world does. The reason I have clumped all these sins together is that they are all a part of the dark and seamy underworld. People in your world may wish that all of you would just go away or die, but I know a better way—that is, that you would meet My Son! We both love you and want to fill you with His and Our Spirit. We know there is a better way for you! There are those of you who have better hearts than those who line the pews of churches. Religious man may fume at what I have just said, but he is always offended by the truth. I do want to clarify one thing, however, for the victims of crime and their friends and families. I absolutely do not ever condone man selfishly hurting man. In fact, I am very, very strongly against it. To the families of children or adults who have been hurt, raped, or killed and to the victims of especially violent crime, I am so very, very sorry for you. I know you have endured a horrible, unbelievably hard ordeal in your lives. I was absolutely not the author of the crime; it was your enemy Satan. Satan is the one who kills, steals, and destroys. I am the one who gives abundant life. You say, "I am God, but I have set up certain rules and laws in the universe." If I broke My own laws, I would die. One of My laws is that when there is sin, there is always an effect from it. You may say, "But I thought Jesus died for sin," and I say, "He did." He died to forgive it, but sin always carries consequences. You might say, "What did my murdered child do to deserve death at the hands of a vicious murderer?" I say, "She did nothing to deserve it, because no one deserves to die like that." However, there can be openings to the devil that leave people susceptible to evil events in their lives. That is why it is so important to learn to pray effectively. You can, by prayer, learn to close the openings to Satan that leave a person wide open to his attacks. It would be better if you went to an intercessor who is skilled in deliverance to learn these prayer secrets, these weapons against the enemy. Every born-again church has people who are prayer warriors. You can call your local born-again, spirit-filled, alive-in-the-spirit church and get help in this area. This is the kind of church you should attend also—a church where they speak in other tongues, have the five-fold ministry working, and, of course, believe in the virgin birth crucifixion, and resurrection of My Son, Jesus.

Then, too, sin opens people up for abuse and crimes, whether it would be the sin of the victim or of generational curses from family sins (even long forgotten). You say, "But I thought Jesus paid for those?" I say, "He did," but there still has to be repentance and obedience, especially in the area of the sin, or the sin still has power over the family. Also,

Satan is a legalistic bully. For him, ignorance of the law is no excuse. He relishes it when he can do a sneak attack against a person.

There is much for you to learn in this area of being protected from the wiles of the enemy, so study your Bibles diligently and find a skilled deliverance intercessor who can help you.

I want to speak now to those who are or have been in prostitution. Have you ever wondered how prostitution began? I will tell you. It came directly from the fall in Eden. When Adam blamed Eve, his wife, and pointed his finger at her and accused her, saying to Me, "the women You gave me," wheels creaked and groaned in realms of spirit. The wheels were part of the "mechanism of horror" that was to follow the fall of man. The wheels were part of "the machine of atrocities" that would rule Earth for a very long time.

Then, far away in time on a lonely hill, an evil Satanic priest ordered a young girl to be raped and then sacrificed to Satan. There was an earthquake at the moment that she was to be killed, and she narrowly escaped certain death. Now, sadly, she was spoiled. The little virgin was now a used and fallen child, and she would be especially in the eyes of the people in her village. There was only one thing she could do now and that was to leave. Staying with the family she loved so much would have assured her death. As she frantically ran away into an unknown world, her mind screamed, "How will I live and eat?" The terrible solution was to be "prostitution." What the evil man of Satan began on the altar of sacrifice was, sorrowfully, to be her life's outcome. Then, long ago, there was a young girl who was taken from her family and enslaved—the same scenario played in her life. And on and on, Adam (the man) hurt "the woman," then sneeringly pointed his finger, and the woman paid the price. For sin always has a price. I know that some girls willingly choose prostitution because they like it, but they are the exception. How many women do you know who would like to have a sweaty, perhaps physically dirty, and unattractive stranger on them doing all manner of gross acts to them? Not many. In fact, that scene smacks of another act: rape! Some distorted men actually believe that women lead them on or enjoy the act of being raped. I say to you, if you truly believe that, you are incredibly deceived. How did you or would you men like to be children again and be viciously raped yourselves? I know many of you were. It didn't feel good, did it?! No, rape is a terrible, unnatural act. It truly hurts and harms its victim, victimizer, and the child it sometimes produces. You men may say, "I was raped as a child and it hurt. Someone has to pay!" I say someone has. Another victim of the awful mess of sin paid—My Son. He paid the price tag that was man's due to pay. If you will let Me teach you, you can be free of all the muck that you have been buried in for so long. For the dirtiness of sin is like quicksand pulling you down into captivity and depraved muddy filth.

To you who are or have been prostitutes (even you males), I know that most of you were abused as children. I know you lost your will to live and that you hated yourselves. I know you are incredibly angry at your abusers and possibly at your mothers, fathers, and families. I know you are rejected by most of society and your families. I know you smoke, drink, and do drugs because of loneliness, hopelessness, and anger. I know the world seems very, very dark to you! And I know for many of you, it truly is dark! But I know something else. I AM Light, and you can be, too! There was a lady named Mary Magdalene. The Bible speaks of her. Jesus knew everything about her. He looked into the "looking glass, the mirror of her soul" with His perceptive revelations. She had seven evil spirits and a spirit of infirmity, and Jesus cast them all out of her. Strange, isn't it, that men who had sometimes been mean to Mary were to be horribly cruel to the One who would save her soul? After

My precious Lamb was resurrected from death to life, it was Mary who was the first to see Him and run to tell His disciples. Mary was His sister now, taken into His family. She was "the chosen of The Most High!" Her past was more than forgotten—It Was Gone, Forever! Mary was absolutely, positively, not the same woman she had been, for she had been reborn! You can be, too! You can be that little girl or boy that I placed into your mother's womb. You can know the deep things of My Kingdom.

No matter what you have done, no matter how horrible the sins you have committed: rape, murder, sexual perversions of all kinds, whatever your sin, I am here to help you get free! I care. I love you! I'll never, ever forsake you. Even if every human on the face of the earth rejects you, I DO NOT! You can be cleaned up, made new and whole. You can be just like Mary Magdalene—the greatest lover of My soul and a truly gentle, loving, and giving helper to people in your world. Does it sound like a miracle? Well, I tell you son or daughter, I Am in the "Miracle Business!" I Am The One Who Created You And I Can and Will Do Absolute Miracles In Your Life—just ask! I love you so.

I want you to know something. When you were little children playing in the sunshine with your dolly or your truck, I saw you. I watched and listened and looked into your sweet little faces and deep inside your hearts. I knew that you weren't depraved Sodomites (from Sodom and Gomorrah). No. You were just little kids. I saw, too, the wretched men who came into you and spoiled and defiled your precious little bodies, and I wept with a father's tears. I want you to know something: You can be washed squeaky clean by the "hovering scrub brush of My Spirit." You can be bright and shiny—brand new.

I know, too, that financial troubles are part of the root of your troubles. I see the terrible money system of your world and I say ... Now Hear This: "This horrible money system which creates so much horrendous suffering of the

peoples of Earth is shortly to be crushed by My Hand!"
There is so much corruption, so much oppression of people,
especially the weak and downtrodden. For when a person
enters a "spiraling down" realm and is caught in a "poverty
whirlpool" and is sucked into the raging, drowning waters
of desolating troubles, no matter how powerful they are,
there is A LIFEGUARD ON DUTY! The lover of your soul is
there with a lifesaver, a lifeboat, and a life jacket. Truly, the
One who loves you and cares is there with LIFE! Just cry
out for help like this, "JESUS, help me!" and We'll be there
in a flash, in an instant, in the blink of an eye. We'll be on
the scene to help you!

Do you know why so many people are dying? So many
are dying because they don't really believe I can or will
help them and because they don't have a vision. Without
envisioning your answer or solution to the problem, which
is the mountain that needs removing from your lives, you
can't have your answer. Do you need a new marriage?
Envision it. See your husband. Do you see him in your
mind's eye? See yourself. Look how happy you both are. See
your family going to the Caribbean. You're all thin, toned,
beautiful. There you are listening to island music on your
great new tape deck, lying next to a gently swaying palm
tree. You can hear the ocean lapping the shore. You are in
heaven. Everything's perfect. That's the picture I desire for
you to have in your spirit and in reality. Ask Me to help you
picture your dreams in living color so that I can give them
to you. It brings Me great joy to see you happy, My precious
little ones. For My heart is yours. My heart beats for you! I
am almost overcome with love. I watch all that you do and I
am smitten with love for you!

SIN IS DIRTY AND DISHONEST

The dirtiness of it creates prime and fertile ground,
which, in turn, grows many things that you do not want in

your life. All manner of filth and impurity are begotten from sin, and sin begets every evil work. Like a chain reaction, sin can start processes or habitual sinning in areas of life. This is how "the Sins of the Forefathers" start. A sin seed is planted in the earth of a person's life. It may be a small thing at first, but then this little seed grows. Just like the mustard seed, one of the smallest seeds on earth, it then becomes a great tree. When sin becomes habitual, then the strong man comes into the house. This spirit is just as the name implies, strong. He is a familiar spirit. He is familiar with your ways. He is like a parasite that worms its way into the flesh and becomes attached with its hooks. This evil spirit becomes so strong and so fixed in a person's life that it actually gets into the genes. Then you have big trouble. For when the genes are penetrated, this evil entity can be passed on to many future generations. When you look at a newborn baby in the hospital, wrapped snugly in a soft blanket, so helpless and gentle, it is hard to believe that he could have sin in his little precious being. Yet wait only about a year or two, and you may see a red-faced, angry little tyrant. You may also see a manipulative, sulking, little child trying every trick to get his own way. This is what sin is: in a word, selfishness. It may be hard to believe, but the seed of sinfulness is resident in that small infant from his conception. The sin that has been passed on to him originated in his parents, Adam and Eve. Just as Adam stole a bite of fruit forbidden by God, which Eve naively offered him, so, too, all who walk the face of the earth have tasted also. You have all sneakily bitten the fruit of evil, sin in all its horror. Sin has a stench, you know. It's a supernatural smell that you can't always smell in the natural because it's in the realm of spirit; however, it can permeate the natural realm, too. Have you ever smelled taverns? Have you ever gone into the bathroom in the morning after a drunkard has been there? Have you ever smelled poverty? The homes of many very poor people smell bad.

However, the worst smell of all is that of Satanism. As these humans enter into the realm of devils, their perversions against Me are a stench that defies description. The smell is literally that of death. For not only do they slaughter the innocents, but they, too, die as they totally rebel against goodness and Me. Their souls and spirits wither and die when they give themselves to this greatest evil. As I watch them, I am so very sorry for them because they have blindly walked into Hell's fires like stupid animals mesmerized at night by a light. In their foolish curiosity and rebellion, they become tools of a gloating devil. He laughs at them like a trapper who has caught an unsuspecting animal in a bag.

Sin is like that; it snares its victim in its jaws, and before the person knows it, he is caught up in it. All sin comes from the same central seed, and that's why I say, if you have committed one sin, you have committed the whole crop of them. This is because when a person sins, he has entered a sin realm where all forms of evil abound. However, there are still degrees of sin. Just as in the physical realm, there are certain kinds of sin that cause cuts or abrasions; there are also those that wound. The wounds, depending upon where they occur in the body and how deep they go, determine the severity of the effect upon the person.

So, too, with sin. It affects, however, the spirit, soul, and body. It takes a heavy toll on not only the sinner, but also on his victim. When sinfulness is birthed, if it is continued in, it will produce victims. Sin victimizes others. It creates wounded, fallen soldiers. It shoots its ugly barbed darts at others as well as at the sinner. It also produces children— the ugly fruits of the original sin. Have you ever noticed how a "little white lie" can sometimes turn into a mess? All it takes is someone hearing about it and a little gossip, and what started as a tiny little fire becomes a raging inferno. That fire burns and hurts its victims, and ultimately, when sin is conceived, it doesn't just hurt, it brings death. This means that when sin is devised or thought about long enough and then acted upon, it conceives and then bears a child of evil. This child is death. Do you know that when you are not overcoming in any area of life, whether it be finances, relationships, health, a peaceful, happy mind or other areas, that you are walking in deception or darkness in that area? That darkness is actually part of the death realm. So when you are being overcome in any area of life, you are actually dwelling in death in that area. What happens when the body dies? First of all, it cannot move and function anymore. Isn't this true of life, too? What happens when a person is very poor? They cannot do the necessary things to get wealth, let alone eking out a pittance of a living. Next, when a person is dead, the light in their eyes goes out. The Bible says all men are lit with the light of God. This is MY energy force that causes man to be able to live. When a person is failing in an area of life, his or her light has ceased to shine into the darkness of that part of their existence. They can no longer discern and make out even the shapes of the components of that realm of life. They are blinded as to how to escape the pitfalls. They stumble and grope in their darkness and miss all kinds of opportunities for deliverance. In this darkness, they become plagued with all the plagues of Egypt. For when sin is conceived, it brings curses, and curses bring the locust. They devour even the good seed. For when the good seed falls on stony ground or is plucked by birds or has no root in it, death follows.

When Pharaoh dared to "thumb his nose" at My servant, Moses, all kinds of curses followed. Locusts came, which were really a spirit of poverty; diseases ravaged his land. All the firstborn were killed, which is the death of children. There was also a plague of frogs, which symbolizes the Satanic realm. All in all, Pharaoh and his nation lost it all. They lost their health, their great wealth, and all joy. Make sure all these woes never happen to you. The waters turned to blood, which is the spirit of war; then there was darkness in the land, which symbolizes total deception and death. Do you know what utter deception is? It is the "reprobate mind," the mind that cannot discern good from evil. The conscience literally dies. In your modern day, you call these people sociopaths.

These people fill the jails. They cannot even feel. They especially cannot feel sorry for their crimes, for their hearts are dead to the pain of others, only to themselves. They are only able to feel their own pain. Eventually, their hearts turn to stone and they then cannot even feel their own pain. This is when they become really dangerous. At that point, it is too late for them (in the natural). They have been drawn into the realm where they believe their own lies—that evil is good and good is evil. Then, all that is left to them is My Spirit. No man can help them. Usually, however, they never wake up from their death sleep because they perceive even Me as evil. Never let your heart become this dead and lifeless. Cry out to Me for deliverance. Go through the pain of life and situations. Do not try to escape it, for then you will die. Remember, you got into your present condition from pain, and it may require pain to be healed, but it is a far better thing to suffer a little while and come out shining with My glory than to remain in old, dead things in old, dead works.

Repent now, before it's too late. Confess your sins one to another. Tell someone you can trust. Ask for their prayers and support. Then turn away from your sin. This will take My help and your prayers beseeching Me to assist you. Repent before your sin blooms in all its horrible glory. Repent while it is still light. For darkness fast approaches on the earth, and repentance will become more difficult, in some ways, because there will be the temptation to try to save your lives whatever the cost.

Antichrist approaches quickly, and the worst sin would

be to be marked by him, to enter the Beast realm for a few pieces of silver. Do not be Judases to Me anymore. For you have all turned away from Me and gone your own way, hurting yourselves and Me.

I say to you, if you are truly Mine, in Me you live and move and have your being. I would that you were absolutely immersed in Me, so that I can protect you, because that is where you are safe. I long to have you tucked snugly under My wing like a mother hen covers her tiny beloved chick.

Repent quickly; time is running out on the "hourglass of the ages" and of your lives. Repent, not just for Me, but also for your own lives that they would not be wasted anymore. Repent that your children might live just as I wish My children to live—abundantly, radiantly, gloriously. I wish that you might live and not die. I wish for you to live life to the very fullest, overcoming, abundant life, the "God kind of life," My life poured out in glory upon you and yours.

THE HEART OF STONE ...

is a cold, hard place, like the moon, pitted with craters. It's dark, lifeless. Can the moon flourish with green gardens and lovely flowing rivers? No. It's dry, a desert, void of life. The heart of a man can be a desert, too. It happens when bitterness enters. The cancerous growth spreads through the chambers of the heart and as it flows and grows, it becomes a deadening "rigor mortis," a dead thing. In this environment, feelings that once could be felt can be no more. Demons have free entrance, and of course, pride is rampant, denying all the while the deadness within. A believer's heart, when it becomes like this, can be harder than the worlds'. At least the worlds' hearts are hard by ignorance, children. Yours are hard by decision. Repent lest any man deceive you. You don't want deception. I warn you strongly: you don't want deception, for in it is death. You want the truth, for in it is light, life, and comfort. I am not giving you a pretty poem. This is serious business. Your life, your children's lives, hang in the balance as never before. The scale is set. You sit on one side. The Devil and his adversaries are on the other.

They are heavy; you are to be light. When you are where you need to be to win the war, your lightness will lift you up out of the scale as the Devil's side crashes to the depths. But it takes real honesty in your life, facing the wrongs you commit, and turning away from wrong. Otherwise, in a very short time, when the world's condition becomes chaotic, you will be snared in a trap, like a fly in a web with a hungry spider nearby. The Devil is hungry. He's hungry for the Word, for families—especially for children, for money. Anywhere there is life, he wants death. Now hear My words. You can win against him, but you must be wise and gentle. To have the wisdom of the serpent and gentleness of the dove requires something of you. You must seek for wisdom in the streets while she can be found. You must turn away wrath and unkindness and do good to your brother. You must give a soft reply and live quiet, peaceable lives. Leave no place open for hardness to enter in. Light the fire of love in your heart. Let it burn away the hard rock. Make it molten, warm, flowing through the chambers of memories, dreams, desires, thoughts, feelings, and especially in your relationship to Me, in a person-to-person way. In fact, start there with you and I, and all else will fall into order.

Old thought patterns, old prejudices, old ways of looking at things will change, because if I say I'll complete you, I will. And I tell you this, I'll do the "greater works" in you. I will. Just wait, you'll see. Though it seems that you've lived and struggled a thousand and one years, there will be a "day in the heights." There will be a day when you reach the summit, look out over green meadows and little dewy flowers. There will be a day where you'll see pristine peaks against bright blue skies; skies that are so beautiful, they almost take the breath away. Pure white, billowy clouds flow across them up to Me in heaven and there We will meet as never before. Your wildest dreams of beauty cannot begin to compare to what you will see and what I have prepared for those who love Me.

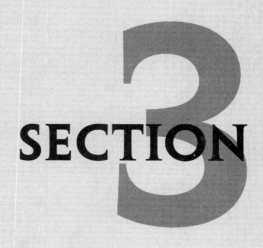

SECTION 3

TO THE FAMILIES OF SATANIC RITUAL ABUSE VICTIMS ...

I am especially writing this letter to those of you who are related to or are even a close friend of a victim of this heinous crime. I want to explain to you just a little of what these poor people have suffered.

For many victims, these terrible crimes against them began when they were little more than babies. As babies, these poor victims did not possess the knowledge of the world that an adult had. They did not have the ability to sift and sort through what was happening to them and come up with logical conclusions, as an older person would. This is true for any child in any given situation. Because children don't possess worldly knowledge, they rely on their feelings. In some respects, this is an adequate way to handle life if there is an adult present who can help nurture them and do the things required for the raising of the child. The adult does have a wisdom about how the world works. This is why I gave children parents.

So first of all, children who were subjected to Satanic ritual abuse had no adult with them who could even try to help them understand what was happening to them. Because of this, these children had to rely on their feelings. Actually, in many respects, children see things more clearly than adults do because fallible human logic doesn't get in their way. So then, in some ways, life's hurts can be more excruciating to a child because he feels it with his whole heart or his emotions, yet cannot logically understand what is behind the pain. This has more of an effect on the spirit man, the eternal part of the person, because these acts of cruelty are not sifted in the mind, but go directly into the spirit-core of the victim.

I do want to state here, clearly, that I have great, great compassion for anyone who has ever, in any way, shape, or form suffered such abuse. I felt your pain so much more

than even you did when you were abused. I feel your pain
now, too, much more than even you do or can imagine.
Believe Me when I tell you this. I weep for you, and I wept
for you. True, there are no tears in heaven, but "My Son, the
intercessor," who is a part of Me, weeps and intercedes for
you on the edge, or rim, of heaven. I tell you, truly, I felt
every pain you suffered because it was literally done to My
Son and hence, to Me before it was done to you. I want to
tell you, I am so sorry that any harm came to your precious
little body, mind, or spirit and I am so extremely sorry for
you. I would not have had one hair on your sweet head
harmed, ever, throughout any of your life. But you live in a
frighteningly sinful world. The corruption of man's heart
would terrify even Me if I were not God. But because I Am
God, I am only saddened by the way men hurt and defile
one another. It is a shameful, horrid thing. It is so contrary
to My nature that at times, I even blush from the terrible
shame of it. I blush that I created creatures that could do
such terrible things! Yet when I have considered wiping out
the human race because of the pain they have caused Me, I
cannot. I repent and turn, even from the deserved judgment,
and lean back onto the "arm of mercy." For I am, in a way, a
slave to My own love. I just love man too much to harm the
whole of humanity. However, the days are coming when I
must exact judgment upon the ungodly. Those who have
abused My little ones must know that they have to repent
thoroughly or be cast, along with hay, wood, and stubble,
into a roaring fire. I do not delight in this. I get absolutely
no pleasure from hurting anyone. However, if they will not
repent, they choose their own path and judgment. They
burn themselves when they will not turn from sin.

Now to you, friends and families of those who suffered
in "the witches' fires" the horror began when many of these
victims were helpless babies. The occult, sneaky as they
always are, spirited these little ones away from their families. These babies were then taken to a place, whether it

was in a countryside, mountainous area, a church, school, or in one of the witches' houses. These babies were usually taken from the security of their homes and were, in the real sense of the word, kidnapped. These darlings were spirited away from all they held dear into a dismal and horrible, beyond-belief, surrealistic nightmarish realm that only a few have tasted of in the earth. In fact, not only have there been only a very limited number of people in the earth who have been the unfortunate victims of this most horrid of all abuses, but most of these victims did not survive it.

After considering what it would be like to be a helpless child and be kidnapped, then think of what it would be like to be in the hands of the worst people your world has to offer. For these are desperately wicked and depraved human beings who know no limit to evil. They are, truly, the worst of the worst. These monsters would make your common serial killer seem like a choirboy. Because they have so completely given themselves over to Satan, they become evil creatures of the night. Your world is full of them. They walk your town's streets. You rub shoulders with them in malls, at the grocery store, at theaters, etc. This Satanic religion is growing by leaps and bounds as people give themselves over to more and more sin in the darkly escalating days as your earth rushes toward the climax of the greatest clash between good and evil.

As the dark witches spy their victim, they converge upon him as if deliciously savoring a good meal. Now they have what they want, what they have been waiting for. They now have free reign to do anything and everything that their own evil hearts could think to do. And as if this wasn't enough, when they can't imagine any more terrible tortures, they will pray to their god, Satan, for his hideous inspiration. Tortures truly beyond your imagination are done to these precious victims. You absolutely cannot imagine what "otherworldly" horrors await these victims in the darkened groves of your earth. So many, many horrendous torments are done to these poor, awaiting innocents in rapid succession that I could not convey to you the immense proportions of the hideousness of the Satanic ritual. I would truly compare these tortures to a person going into Hell. In one aspect, they are even worse. When a person is in Hell, they are in their spirit body, not in a natural physical body, so that they cannot have tortures done to them in quite the same way. The physical pain during the rituals is utterly unbearable. Many of the victims die from the pain alone. Prison camp experiences or ancient tortures in dark dungeons would pale in comparison to the rituals. Then, there is the terrible sexual abuse. Even the term "sexual abuse" sugarcoats the reality of what the victim suffers. There are no adequate human words to describe the physical or sexual abuse. I will not honor Satan by going into detail; just believe this: unless your eyes have seen these horrendous sexual tortures, you cannot even begin to imagine the depths of depravity to which humans could sink.

Many of the victims die the most atrocious deaths imaginable. They die from slow methodical tortures, from painful, sadistic rapings, and from the sights they must watch as other victims are brutalized. These poor unfortunate people die the most horrible deaths your planet has to offer. All other deaths pale in comparison to these, except for My Son's death. They die from untold physical pain. They die from shock, from what they witness, and from the horrors that are heaped upon them and what they are forced to watch, or even do, to the other victims. And sometimes, their sweet bodies just quit, give up, from the trauma and terrible sorrow of what is inflicted upon them. So few people can survive these sordid rituals. Ultimately, it is only by My Spirit that a person could survive such utter desolation, because, in reality, the brutalizing is so complete and so horrific that no one could survive except by My command, by My Spirit. Any victim who has survived the deathly rituals is indeed a survivor of the finest kind.

Truly, the prison camp victim's experiences in Auschwitz (Nazi prison camps) would, in comparison, be like a couple of drops of water in a bucket when compared to the full bucket of Satanic ritual abuse. They would pale in comparison to this most hideous of all sufferings. Did you notice that most of the words I use to describe this Satanic crime begin with the letter "H?" Interesting, isn't it, that horrible, hideous, horrific, horrid, horrendous, heinous, etc. all begin with the same letter as Hell. And believe Me, the rituals are the earth's Hell. They are truly Hell on earth.

I have not even covered the spiritual aspect of what the Satanists and Satan himself inflict upon their victims. It is, by far, the worst part. If the coven is at all practiced in the "dark arts," the spiritual and emotional torment and damage they can inflict is unbearable and unbelievably hellish for the victims. Weird and horrible mind games are played with the poor victim. They are told many terribly tormenting lies and in their weakened physical state from the tortures, they usually believe them. Then, weird religious rituals of all kinds are done. Many of the cult's religious ceremonies and techniques are unified. These could include voodoo, Druidism, and other religious rituals. Ancient religions are studied by members of the coven as well as the Satanic orders of other countries.

Then, there are the drugs. The poor victim may be given drugs in powder form, to be inhaled or mixed into food or drink, or drugs given by injection or in recent times with a skin patch. Also, drugs can be given by even a prick on the finger or body. These drugs can include powerful mind-altering hypnotics or disease-inducing drugs; drugs that can be crossed with other drug compounds to produce horrible reactions or even allergic reactions in the body. Wild toxins are sometimes given to the victim that can cause a quick, or worse yet, lingering, horrid death. Alcohol is sometimes used, as are sedatives to quiet or put the victim to sleep quickly.

I could go on and on. For I have not really told you the specifics of all that Satanists do to people. For yours and the victims' protection, I will not go into specifics, but as you can see, Satan has a large and varied arsenal. Consider what it would be like to be in the bowel, the belly of Hell, and have the demons tormenting you. First, one would strike, then in rapid succession another and another with a variety of different torments. This is what the Satanic ritual is often like. However, in the earth, men have to breathe, and being tortured so constantly hardly gives the victim enough chance to catch his breath.

Just believe your God. If you have never suffered this otherworldly torment, you cannot fully comprehend it, regardless if you have counseled victims for years or been closely related to them or been a close friend. For if words almost fail Me to tell of the effects of Satanism, surely men are also limited in understanding the depths of depravity to which the Satanists go. Just agree with Me that you cannot even begin to comprehend the utterly unbelievable, hideously horrible fate that the victims of Satanism suffer.

Due to the suffering of the victims of Satanic ritual abuse, what fate do you think would befall anyone who would knowingly further harm any of these victims who have endured Hell's fires? Doesn't My Word state that, "I will not bruise a broken reed?" If I won't, you cannot either. I, the God of All, will not permit any of these little ones to be hurt further. Oh, you may, for a time, be able to punish and hurt them, but there is a great price for your torment. Unless you repent, absolutely, with restoration to the person and with godly sorrow and strong tears (complete repenting), you will burn, too. For when you further torment these victims, you become as one of the Satanists.

So, the choice is yours: repent completely or suffer the consequences. These people need all the love and compassion the world has to offer them. They have survived Hell's torment. They were stripped of their homes and families, many of them alone, out in what should have been to them peaceful, beautiful forests. Many were there, standing in the place of their families, who the Satanists constantly threatened to murder, without the victim's compliance—and the Satanists would have done just that. They were there alone, stripped of their dignity, humiliated and naked and almost assured of a horrible death. Those who did survive were, in some ways, the most unfortunate, for they had to carry on with their lives: going to school, church, jobs. Many of these lost friends or potential friendships because they were perceived as being weird. Many of these suffered illnesses and all manner of nervous conditions as well as mental troubles. Many were inflicted with lifelong physical wounds from the tortures. These poor people are many times condemned to lives hardly worth living. Even if they are healed by Me, they still have lost so very, very much: their virginity, their innocence, their childhood, and their sense of well-being— the feeling that they are safe and living in a happy world.

I would that you would minister to these people who have endured "life's cross," who have suffered the most closely to My Son. In fact, some of them actually have been "crucified" by the occult by literally hanging on crosses, just like the greatest of all of the "survivors of the occult, Jesus." For when My Son died, He, too, died at the hands of Satanic men, those under the control of Satan.

If you have survived Satanic ritual abuse, know this: I am here to heal you and I will. Know this, too: As your blood cries out, I will avenge those who have harmed you unless they repent.

TO YOU, WHO HAVE BEEN IN WITCHCRAFT AND THE OCCULT ...

I know the evil of your ways. They are not new or frightening to Me. For at the end of My Book, Satan is cast into the "Lake of Fire" that shall burn him and those who are with him forever. I do not desire to cast you into the melting, searing, fiery torment that was created not for humans, but for the enemy.

Unknown to you as you practice your craft and kill and maim My little ones, I weep and mourn for you as well as for them. For you are victims of the devil, too. He uses you at will and shall one day cast you away as a piece of used up garbage. You are a pawn in his sinister game, which is aimed as much at you as at your victims.

Even so, My arms are open wide for you. I long to deliver you from evil and bring you the joy you have tried so long to find. I know your longings and confusion. I know you don't know where you are going or what to do with your life. I know many of you have children and families and some of you hide your sin from them. Some of you have hurt your families, even your beautiful children. Please know that you will not gain favor with Satan by harming children, adults, or animals. He just laughs and mocks you behind your backs. He knows he has trapped yet another person, a fly in his web, and he calls you "a fool."

But to Me, you are not a fool; you are a person who has been deceived by evil. I have not turned My back on you even though My heart breaks at what you do.

Very soon, judgment will fall upon those who practice wickedness. Please, get out of the way of the wrath that is coming upon the children of disobedience. My arms are still open to you. I have not turned away from you, but someday I must if you will not repent. So do not wait! There is little time. You could be picked off by the enemy this very day or night as you sleep soundly and go down, down into the pit of torment and torture. Think how you would feel if "you" were one of "your" victims and of Satan's. Think of the agony that you have perpetrated on others returning multiplied to you. That is the plan of the enemy for you. And even if you have never hurt or killed another, by your sin of participating in any way in the occult, even innocently playing the Ouija board, Dungeons and Dragons, Tarot cards, tea leaves, séances, trances, horoscopes, or any other form of occult or witchcraft activity, you have done it all. Even a seemingly small sin in this area is participating in a great evil. My Word says, "He who is guilty of one sin is guilty of all."

I am very strongly against this area of sin. I must solemnly warn you!

Please, please put away childish foolishness and come to the One who wants you and can make all things right for you in your lives.

My arms are open wide to you still. I want to forgive you and restore your life.

TO ALL YOU WHO HAVE DONE CRIMES ...

been involved in drugs, murdered, raped, or hurt others or yourselves, know this—I was there and watched it all. I cried for your victim and for you, too. You hurt yourself and your own soul more than you hurt your victim, and that is a very sad thing. You both became the losers. No one won. Even if you were not caught, your sin will find you out and catch up to you!

Come to Me, let Me help you. I am able enough to carry you in My strong yet gentle arms. I know many of you abusers have been abused. It is time to break the cycle, isn't it? You do not have to be a slave to sin.

Drugs do not have to be your slavemaster. I am the "Master." I have authority over the spirit behind drugs, that spirit of control and destruction.

And to you, thieves, liars, and all manner of sinful people, I came into the world in My Son, Jesus, to set you free and break the chains that I see upon you in the spirit.

I love you. More than anything in the world, I want you all to know you are loved and cared for. I know that through these letters to you, I keep repeating that, but I must make that one thing clear. If you only know that I love you, then I have succeeded. I love people everywhere.

I am here for you, waiting to hear you ask Me to help you. I am ready to, in an instant, rescue you, Do not delay. Deadly forces want you, too. Don't let them take you from My waiting arms!

TO YOU WHO HAVE DONE EVIL ACTS...

with your own sex or have done other wicked perversions, I tell you, I hate your sin mightily, yet I love you still. I especially hate the sin of perverted sex because it hurts so many. It is a completely unnatural affection. It is out of the order of all I have created. It destroys so many lives—not only of the victims and of the victimizers, but also those around them. It is impure, unholy, and is a mockery and counterfeit of all I have planned for the family on the earth.

My plan was for a man and his wife to have children and to live a joyous, quiet, simple life. Does that sound boring to you? That is because you have never felt the peace and joy of serving Me and also the exhilaration and thrill of what I long to reveal to My people—things too wonderful and glorious that you know not.

Yet in spite of the children whom some of you have hurt terribly and the men and women who have been your victims, I am still here, ready to forgive and forget.

I implore you, turn from evil before it's too late. It is not My desire to have to hurt any man. There is a "seat of mercy as well as a seat of judgment in heaven." Please, please, do not come to Me at the seat of judgment, but rather, come to Me where I sit in tender mercy for you.

Ask Me now to help you repent of your sins. Do this in faith, whether you feel sorry or not, believing that I will help you to turn from your wicked ways.

The time is short before those in perversions are judged. Do not delay! Seek wise Christian counsel, if necessary.

Don't be afraid. I will never reject you, even if humans do.

"Come unto Me all you who labor and are heavy laden and I will give you rest."

YOU ARE THE HEAD AND NOT THE TAIL

The tail is a very real place, just as the head is. It is a place on the body that you do not want to live in. It is a smelly, foul part of the anatomy. It is useful because it is for one purpose—elimination—but it is not an area where I want My children to dwell. It stinks! In dogs, worms and parasites come out of the area of the tail, as do the useless remains of the food they have eaten.

Think of the tail in spiritual terms. It is the last place on the body that a person would want to be. Being in the tail is to be a loser—at the bottom instead of the top. It is being last instead of first. Being a spiritual loser is the worst place on earth to be, because all physical things proceed out of the spiritual. Foul-smelling air is eliminated from the tail, polluting even the atmosphere around it. So, too, in the spiritual realm. It is a dark and dirty, smelly place to live. Many people live in just such surroundings. Check yourself! What kind of home do you live in? Are you overwhelmed by life? Are you living in victory or defeat?

The head is the first; it is the top. The head has a brain. It can think and feel. It is not mindless, as the tail is. It can problem solve. It can dream. It can have faith. The head can also hear My word and beautiful music and act upon it. It can see beauty with its eyes. The head can smell the per-fumy fragrances of the earth. But, best of all, the head can speak and create with the tongue, just as I do. The head is the place of anointing. It is the place of beginnings. I say again, "It is the place of new beginnings!"

Some of you are so used to being in the tail that you believe that it's where you should be. It seems normal and natural to you. Perhaps your parents lived there, too. Did they live in poverty, spiritual poverty, not possessing enough of My spirit to have victory in their lives? Did they live in financial poverty, living in lack? Did they always struggle and never have enough, especially more than enough to help many others? Were their storehouses empty and lacking? Were they or their children living in sickness? Were their teeth whole and well? Did they have a nice home to raise their children in and all the necessities of life plus much more to share with others? Were they well mentally, or were they worried or depressed? Did they have to bear up under heaviness and burdens? Were their children healthy, happy, and prosperous? Were your parents spiritually overflowing in the knowledge of who I AM? Were they full of My Spirit and in touch with Me? Were they walking in overcoming joy and faith?

If you can't answer these questions in the affirmative, the chances are you don't possess all these things yourself. You may say, "But there is a place of suffering in this world." It's true, but I say, "In this world you will have tribulation (problems, suffering) but ... the good news is, son, daughter, be of good cheer, be of good cheer, for I, Your Daddy, Your Father, have overcome, beaten, won over, been victorious, overcome the world, and so have you." Many of My children have drunk of the dregs, the bottom of the barrel, the woes of this world. Many of Mine have lived in the dark, musty dungeons of the earth. Saint Paul lived in a dungeon for part of his natural life, but he did not truly live there; he lived in glory.

My Word says, I wish above all things that thou might prosper and be in good health, even as your soul or mind prospers. These areas, first your finances, your health and your mind, are the areas Satan loves to attack. He understands that he can wreak havoc in your life, marriage, and family by attacking these key areas. Adam and Eve lived in paradise. They had it all. They were prosperous because they possessed everything they could have ever needed or wanted. They were in perfect health and they were perfectly happy and content. That was what the fruit was all about. They were tricked into believing they needed something they didn't possess—a piece of forbidden food. I do not want My children tricked in any way by Satan. I want you to live in paradise, too. I want you to have all the goodness of paradise. You may live in a messy world, not in Eden, but I can help your life to become an Eden even in the midst of a tempestuous world. I want to deliver your life from grimness and the death of sin. I want to deliver you out of the murky places, the smoldering ashes so many of Mine have lived in and thought to be "natural" for so long.

I want to restore and heal the dry, parched bones. I want to rehydrate them by My Spirit. This is the time of the restoration, the repairing of the breach, the broken. You who are broken in two, you who are bone-weary, who don't know which way to turn, you are the ones I desire to heal by My Spirit. I long to and will make you the head, the first, the top.

Worship Me for this great restoration. I know your petitions, your prayers. Now worship and praise Me for the answers to them. Thank Me for healing all your and your families' lives. I am the victorious one! I am a winner, and you are, too. Act like it, even before it happens. Quit telling people how broke you are or how sick you are or how you aren't going to make it! Settle it in your heart that you are going to overcome in great glory and great victory in all areas of your life. Say what I say; be glad that I only speak good things because I hold all in My hand. If I spoke evil, evil would happen. It is so with you, too! Speak things that are not as if they already are. Talk victory! Talk solutions; talk dreams; especially talk and speak about dreams and hopes. Ask Me to give you new dreams, if you need them.

We are victors together. You are not alone and helpless. You have Me. Worship Me for the new good thing I will do in your life. Praise Me for making you the head and not the tail!

MONEY

Have you ever wondered why I created money? Adam and Eve never needed money in Eden. So then, money was a part of the curse. That is not to say that money is cursed. On the contrary, money is a blessing. In Eden, Adam and Eve were supernaturally provided with everything they needed. It was such a lovely, comforting way of life. Even their tending the Garden and the naming of the animals was joyous. It was the ministry of being an overseer, a king. They were the rulers of the Garden of Eden! But then the tempter of their souls was sent into paradise so that I could judge their hearts. I wanted to place My stamp of approval upon them and say, "Well done," but, alas, they did not do well, and they fell from grace. They had to be cast out of their heavenly home to keep them from living forever in their fallen state. My heart broke more than theirs because I looked down through the ages and foresaw the corruption of mankind. But then I was ready with a backup plan, not "My first fruits Perfect Will Plan," but "My Second Fruits Plan," My Son's gift of life. For I devised the two beauties of Eden to succeed and to populate the earth. Heaven on earth was to be My grand design. But man's heart was found to be corrupt. When the two were cast out of Eden, they entered a cold and lonely world. They would soon discover just how oppressive the dark land they had entered would be. Suddenly, they were not cocooned in a soft, warm, and fuzzy place, but an alarm clock buzzed and clanged, "Time to get up and go to work." Now Adam had to work and work very hard. It was hot and dirty, and he sweated profusely.

Now I could fully see man's heart. It was so able to do wrong, so contrary to Me. I knew I had to create a way for mankind to live in a "survival-of-the-strongest world," so I created a means of exchange: money. I could not trust men to be fair and kind to one another, for man was concerned about one thing—himself! Money was the only answer to man's sinful nature. However, I always bring beauty out of ashes! I knew that I could bless and reward people for good deeds with money. For those religious people who proudly say they do not need money, I challenge them to try to get along without it for a week. Your world revolves around finances. My Word speaks of money more than any other subject because of its importance to you. Most crime is done because of mammon. I say it is the root of all evil, because even if money is not always directly involved in an evil deed, its sister, "power," is. For greed and lust are the other children of the desire for riches. Not that it is evil to desire money. You need it desperately in your fallen world. Rather, it's when you love money, especially when you love it more than Me, that it becomes your wife, your god. I say I will have no other gods ruling My children's hearts. Only I will sit on your heart's throne. I will do whatever it takes in your life to ascend the stairs to the throne room of your spirit! I do not do this to hurt you, but rather to save you from yourselves. I love you with a sweet and gentle mother's heart. The fatherly part of Me may have to be firm, but I always love you sweetly and mercifully, for I AM "The Breasted One." As "The Breasted One," I feed you the sweetness of the milk of the Word, but I also pour out of Myself blessings and rewards.

In the days ahead, money will be sucked out of men's hands and piled up into the hands of evil little men. The Antichrist will be skilled at manipulation as he sways continents, countries, and kings with gold and silver. He will dangle a carrot in his mouth, tempting the rulers of men to bite of it. Just as Satan impressed Adam and Eve to take a bite of disobedience, so, too, will the Antichrist.

There is a portion of My Spirit in money. Don't I speak of the Holy Spirit as oil? The fragrant anointing oil was the most valuable thing in the world in ancient times. Wine was also valuable. These were words I used to describe the

Holy Spirit's attributes: fragrant, intoxicating. So it is with riches. Riches can be a great blessing. They can take you to faraway lovely places and buy beautiful homes and cars. Riches can be bestowed upon you and your children in the form of fine clothing, education, wonderful food, healthy nutritional products, vacation fun, etc. The list goes on and on. All these things are necessary parts of life in your world. Try living without them and you will suffer. So, too, without Me and My Spirit, you will not live life to its fullest. It is a package deal. You need it all to be truly happy in life. It is just the way it is. It is a practical plan I created to make a fallen world tolerable, and yes, joyous.

Don't I say in My Word, "I wish above all things that thou might prosper and be in good health even as thy soul prospers?"

The first thing I wish for you is that you would prosper. I wish this above everything else because you have need of it so desperately. You need prosperity first for survival, then for joyousness, then to set the captives free. People are watching you. They are thinking one of two things: look at those poor Christians in their old car, drowning in debts. I don't think I want to be one of them if they have a poor God. Or they look at you and say to themselves, God is really blessing this family. They lack for nothing wonderful, in fact, they seem to get all the goodies. They serve an awesome God. This is not to say that I desire men to come to Me for what they can "weasel out" of Me, but rather for love. However, I do reward obedience and committedness.

I did create My little ones to rule and reign with Me in Heaven and the universe. Your instruction to be a ruler, a king and a priest in the order of Melchizadek must begin now. I say again—it must begin now. You are now in the school of the eternal. You are learning heavenly things now in your present life. Your spirit will carry these nuggets of gold into eternity, where more riches will be added to them. Besides, I created planet Earth for you to rule and reign over, but not as rich little dictators. No, that is the way the Beast would run things. I made My children to be kind, loving, giving rulers of the earth, just like Me. I created you to be "little Jesuses." My precious sons, lovely brothers and sisters, full of tender mercies and compassion for a lost and dying world. Your world needs to see a family of "gentle monarchs" who are receiving their Father's greatest wish, that is, prosperity, good health, and a sound and joy-filled mind. I say again, I wish above all things under heaven and above earth and through all universes that you would prosper and be in good and glorious health in your sweet body and that your mind would be filled with heaven's splendor. I desire that you have it all, that you want for nothing in your life.

My Word says, "The wealth of the wicked is poured out on the righteous in the end days," and so the wealth shall be given into the hands of men, men whom I can trust with it, men who will share and not be greedy, men who can see the bleeding, hurting heart of humanity. As the hour grows more desperate and people are watching their loved ones die from killer diseases and unimaginable poverty, the world will be frantically looking for an answer. They will have two choices: the evil one or you. In the desperation of the hour that is quickly approaching, kings and princes will run to My children's light to implore their help. Yes, whole countries will be crying out, " Save us, save our babies," and you will answer as if from heaven, "I am here, God's messenger, God's emissary." The Holy One has heard your hearts' cry. He cares, he longs, to help you. He sends me in His place to be a tender lamb, a sweet anointing oil to you, a covering to your nakedness, a gentle dove. I will cradle your little ones in my arms. I will anoint their sweet heads with the oil of promise. I will dry the tears from the mother's eyes in your land. I will be a repairer of the broken. I will be a comforter to you and your people. I will give to you from My Father's tender heart. I will bestow upon you kindness and the mercies of God!

Ultimately, I want to bless you so that you can bless many from your overflow, from your excess. I long to open Heaven's windows and pour out from My Father's heart treasures that are so great you cannot contain them. Heavenly treasures that will spill onto men who are hot and thirsty and who will drink them up as dry, hardened sponges suddenly plunged into cool, clear water—sponges regenerated, softened, brought from death to life. These are the dry bones that lie death-like in the valleys of the earth. They cry out for water to be rehydrated so they can arise from dryness into newness of life. For I am the restorer and the repairer of all the broken, of all who mourn in Zion. I long to set men free to worship Me in the beauty of holiness. I long to restore and I take great joy in elevating My children to new heights of the Spirit and the natural earthly realm as well. I long to put you on display for the world and show the people of earth the splendorous beauty that I can create in My people's lives.

Cry out to Me with loud crying, especially you fathers, for you are the overseers of your families. Implore Me to bless you and yours, for I am the Breasted One. I control the oil, the wine, the milk, and the honey and I surely own the cattle on a thousand hills. For you who think you are doing "all right" financially, soon, unless you grab ahold of Me and My Words on prosperity, you won't be! For the world and you are shortly to be plunged into financial darkness, gloomy and frightening, unless you have My light. Then you shall be light to a darkened world and seasoning salt to a bland and lifeless earth. You shall perk up all that you touch, and you shall literally restore life to a dying planet. For you, too, will be the oil that restores and gives new breath to man.

Repent quickly for the sins of foolishness and folly in the ways you have misused and selfishly squandered the money I have given you. Repent and then forget past mistakes and ask Me for new wisdom and a new day of financial anointing for you and yours in the days ahead so that you might be a blessing to a world that awaits your rulership.

MEMORY IN THE BLOOD!

All people who are born are the product of their genetic blueprints. You have been produced from genetic codes that have made you unique, yet are product of your heritage, your bloodline. For when you were birthed from a woman, you could not escape your genealogy. For many of you, it would definitely have been better if you could have. Most of you, dear ones, did not come from the "crème de la crème" of humanity. On the contrary, you were propagated from "barbarians." The world was especially barbaric in ages past. You have only to consider how your ancestors ate their food to arrive at the fact that man is a base creature only recently civilized. Many of your ancestors dined like swine and then threw their half-eaten bones to their dogs. Best not even to imagine the coarse bathroom habits and gross sexuality of many peoples and cultures, too. The brutal birthing process has also been an earthly reality of life. Consider the grossness of parasites that plague humanity. Imagine the stench of plagues and illnesses, and the terror of unnatural things, such as abortion, let alone all manner of confinements in jails and institutions, and it is easy to see how human and how gross are your springs from whence you've sprung. The whole of the human quandary would be funny if it weren't so very sad. If I did not have a father's heart, the seed that you came from would have been blotted out long ago. Yet even in the disgusting elements of life, I have the restorer's heart. I bring beauty from the ash heap of the fire of your life. For many of you, your hearts have been a cold place. The fire long ago went out in your hearts. Your family's long-forgotten pasts have played their evil tunes right down through the ages into yours and your children's lives. For truly, the Blood does Remember. Yes, the blood of you and your kin remembers old, ancient things. Though you may not consciously remember your family history, the "life in the blood" does remember. It has been coded with curses and with blessings—curses and blessings visited down onto unsuspecting generations.

To look at a newborn baby, one would not suspect all that is encoded into the infant. Yet it is chockfull of humanity—other people's humanity. For that baby carries generations in his blood. Whether that blood is full of blessings or woes is a matter of genealogy.

For some of you who were with Me before the foundations of earth were formed, you had a choice of families; however, it was not much good to you because man is born into sin. So you, too, had to leave heaven and be placed inside a sinful woman just as your brother Jesus was. It was not pleasant at times, this being carried in a Womb of Sin. Yet there would be things that would help compensate. Just seeing the light of a new day would comfort many of you and let you know someone cared enough to let you smell the fresh morning air and rejoice. Still, man had to be let out of the squalor of humanness, and only a miracle could change the Memory of the Blood. Something supernatural was needed to deliver humankind.

Only then could the blood's memory cells be changed from evil to good.

How strange it was that when a tiny baby boy was birthed in a stable, His Blood would blot out the transgressions that were carried in the blood of the human race. His birth could be likened to a seemingly insignificant event that could have happened in your lifetime. In modern terms, it would be as if a couple were traveling a long distance because their government insisted that they appear in the state capital to register for the census. The couple was not poor. As a matter of fact, the wife was from a wealthy family and her husband had a good business in carpentry and construction. The sweet young woman was pregnant, yet she didn't complain. As they drove into town, they noticed that so many people were there, just like them, trying to get to the state building to sign a lot of papers. They wondered why there had to be such a bureaucratic hierarchy that made people feel like common animals. The young woman was so gentle and kind. As they neared the capital building, Mary felt a twinge of pain. She said nothing, yet hoped they'd be able to leave soon. However, that was not to be the case.

After standing in a long line of people for many hours, their turn finally came. Mary silently thanked God. After signing all the dismal paperwork, Joseph took his wife's arm. He looked tenderly at her and noticed how tiny and delicate she was. How sad, he thought, to see his precious wife so great with child, so uncomfortable, yet so brave. However, he was comforted as he thought about the hotel, warm bath, and good dinner that they would shortly have. But as they entered the city, every inexpensive motel had a "full" sign out in front. No matter, they always stayed in the best ones anyway. But after several hours of driving all over town, they realized that every place was full. What to do? Then, in horror, Joseph looked at Mary's face and saw pain on it. "Oh no, this can't be happening," he thought. "Maybe it's false labor." Then Mary groaned and told Joseph her water had just broken. Joseph drove quickly to a hospital, but when he entered the emergency room, he was told there had been a terrible train accident and all the hospitals were completely swamped. Joseph ran to the car and frantically told his child-bride that they would have to try to find someone who could help them.

Now Mary was in real pain, and Joseph was scared. He drove, not really knowing where he was going. He was in the country now. In front of them was a big farmhouse. He knocked on the door and a kind lady appeared. Joseph told her of their predicament, and the lady graciously offered them her barn because she had a house full of people. Then Joseph ran out to his wife and carried her quickly into the barn out in the backyard. Mary protested because she didn't want her husband to hurt his back. He gently placed her onto some clean straw and ran inside to call a doctor, but all of them were busy treating victims of the train wreck. Joseph knew, at that moment, that it was just he and his wife. The baby took many hours to be born, but with Joseph's help, a crying child came into a cold barn one glorious night. The surroundings were so humble.

Then, when Joseph went outside to get a breath of air, there was a huge star blazing in the royal blue sky. He had never seen a star so bright. The rays of light that proceeded from it seemed to engulf the barn. He wondered at it. Suddenly, down the road he saw some men in a Rolls Royce. The three men got out of the beautiful car and came toward Joseph. They were dressed in the most elegant clothes that Joseph had ever seen. They looked as if they were straight off the Paris runways. "These men were rich, really rich," Joseph thought. As they neared him, Joseph saw their faces. They were the most dignified and the kindest looking men he had ever seen. What happened next amazed Joseph. The three men told him they had seen the star in their own part of the country and had followed its rays to the barn. They were there to worship a king, they excitedly told Joseph. Then Joseph remembered what the angel had told him about the royal child his wife would have, the one who would save mankind. Still, Joseph didn't really comprehend completely what the meaning of the angel's message was. He then led the three men into the barn and presented them to his wife, but when they caught sight of the baby, they fell to their knees in adoration. Joseph was incredulous as he watched the strangers begin to cry. Exhausted, Joseph began to cry, too. He sobbed into his hands, and Mary gently patted his arm. His wife was quiet and peaceful, but

Joseph saw something in her eyes. He couldn't quite detect what it was, but it caught his heart. Then the men each took a beautifully wrapped gift out of their coat pocket and placed it beside the baby. Mary graciously accepted the gifts and was amazed to see a large gold nugget in one and in the other, two vials containing the most beautiful spices: frankincense and myrrh. The strangers then said they had to leave, but as they got up to go, a group of ranchers came through the barn door and when they saw the child, began praising God. A celebration of praise was offered for this gift to men. Little did they know then that the blood of man that remembered sin would be washed by the Blood of the tiny baby who lay sleeping peacefully in his mother's arms.

How strange that such a seemingly usual birth could change the world. Yet in a moment in time, humankind would be changed forever. For what had failed in a Garden would succeed in a stable, now that the second Adam had been birthed. For at Calvary, man's sins were nailed to a cross and stamped by the hand of God, "PAID FOR, NO DEBT, NOT GUILTY." From that moment into eternity, the blood of men could rejoice and be changed from evil generations into a new overcoming power. For now, the serpent had been trampled and man could look toward heaven and know without doubt that there was no more curse. Men could, with no fear, bask in the warmth of the Father's love. For now, their blood guiltiness was changed into snowy whiteness. Now mankind could relax and know who their God was without wondering what God thought of them. For now, they understood what the prophets of old had said, "But He was wounded for our transgressions. He was bruised for our iniquities; the chastisement of our peace was upon Him; and with His stripes we are healed." No need now to fear the blood, for the putrid blood of men had been redeemed by a pure white lamb, and the Glory of His Preciousness had made man acceptable and greatly desired by God.

SECTION 4

THE HEALING OF THE MIND

Do you realize that when the emotions or the mind is damaged that there is always a resulting brain disorder, hence, brain damage? Most people and physicians would anticipate brain damage when there is an injury to the cranium or spinal cord. However, very few would believe that permanent brain damage could come from emotional woundings. You see, the woundings of the emotions are a real thing, physiologically speaking.

Childhood traumas and hurts literally affect the brain. When a person is wounded by another or by themselves, the chromosomes are affected. They become rearranged. The neurons misfire and eventually, if the wound is not dealt with, there is the ultimate cell death. The scientists will discover all this shortly.

However, in their blindness, they won't know what to do with this information. For their minds are as narrow as their science. Hear this: "Many of the silly, little, boxed-in scientists can only think silly, little, boxed-in thoughts." For if they cannot prove a theory, it must surely be false. This is so sad. Science must be linked with My Mind to excel. As long as these scientists look to their own theories, in their old stagnant ways, they will be crippled.

There are a number of ways to heal the brain—all depend on My mercy and power to redeem. One would be prayer. Another, a machine that literally smoothes the brain; another, nutrition. Then there are the aromatic oils, counseling, surgery, and being in My presence. The scientists will shortly try new and unusual drugs, rays, and techniques to heal the mind. Some will help; others will have disastrous consequences. Did you know that for many of you, the root of your trouble is genealogical? The root of your problem is an actual ancestor of yours. For instance, many of you had a relative, far back in your lineage, who loved the sweet rich, dainties of Egypt. This produced blood sugars that went wild, first low and then high blood sugar (diabetes). Tooth decay and emotional yo-yos were then brought into your family, then eventually, depression and suicide spirits. Chain reactions literally put chains around your necks, and you and your kin became captives. For many others of you, witchcraft entered your bloodlines, especially in the Dark Ages and oh, the agony it has caused you and yours. All these sins and so many more sifted down through generational times and affected you. Your very genes (taken from the root word genealogy) became changed and affected. The life force, the bloodlines, were truly changed. The blood and body chemistry are actually affected by sin as well as goodness, even through the generations. What your great, great, great grandfather did affects you today, not only physically, but mentally and in the Spirit Realm as well.

Many people teach that all you have to do is rebuke the problem, but for heavy, long-standing sins, which became curses, which became the "Woes of God," a little rebuke is not enough. There is more to it than that. There must be complete repentance for the sin. That means that you are sorry for hurting, first your God, then others, and then yourself. You need to ask for forgiveness for the person who first committed the crime against Me. And then, lastly, after praying My Son's blood over the iniquity, you must walk out the obedience or turning from the sin. If you stumble, you repent and begin the process again. And so you do what I have just told you again and again. No matter how many times you must repeat the process, just do it. You may need someone else who is knowledgeable to help you, especially in the case of heavy, sordid sins that seem to stick like glue. Eventually, though, when you have learned your life's lesson, you will be delivered. When you truly discover "the way" and realize that the sin wasn't even that great or that much fun and that there is something better, you will be cleansed.

Besides, I'll always give you a gift much more fulfilling than the sin.

I want a clean, unshackled people. Most of you are such prisoners! Almost each and every one of you sits in a dimly lit cell. It's dank, dreary, and dark. The rats (the dark forces) love it there. They are so familiar with the prison walls that enclose you. Their highest aim is to keep you there and then send you to death row.

But praise will break you free from the shackles. Praise Me all day long and in the night hours. Let joy be upon your heart and love for Me be upon your tongue.

It's not easy to fight the wickedness of your world alone, but it is easy when you give yourself over to Me. When all else fails, praise never fails because praise is the high form of love. If you want your brain cells healed and your life healed, just thank Me. Tell Me you love Me, not for Me, but for you, because the enemy cannot dwell in the hallowed Holy Place of the sweet-incense-odors of praise. Mystery, wonder, and glory are the wafting, sweet mountain-of-spice praises of God's people. There is the hidden place beneath My wing where all the plagues of Hell and humanity cannot touch you. There is the shadow of the Most High God. There is the armor, the bloodshed abroad, the all-overshadowing, all-encompassing place of deliverance. There, we meet cheek-to-cheek, Spirit-to-Spirit.

Just ask Me to show you how to praise Me, to show you the way. New forms of praise will become so incredible and different that you will hardly believe what you are about to see.

As the enemy of your souls bolsters up his forces to a furor, so, I, too, am just about ready to declare nuclear war on Satan. The sound of horses' hooves is fast approaching. The coming hoofbeats of My Crystal White Son with hair of wool and a sharp sword in His mouth is shortly to stampede your planet, and all shall know there is a God and many will be delivered. So prepare yourself, My Chosen

Bride, for your true love's arrival. Adorn yourself in the "garment of praise for the spirit of heaviness," and then live and abound in an abundance of life.

Many of you may be tempted to believe you can fight what is coming in your own power. If you have never believed anything else before, believe this: You cannot fight the coming clash, the holocaust dead ahead. Only in Me will you ever survive and, better yet, overcome. For in Me, you can win the war of all wars.

THE TREE OF BITTERNESS ...

is bitter indeed. It hurts people: the person who's bitter, the object of his bitterness, and others.

The roots of it go deep into the very depths of the person. If you could see it as I do, you would see an ugly, nasty tree, full of thorns and bitter-as-gall fruit. For it does produce fruit, just like other fruit trees. The color of the tree is black—dismal and dreary. When a person goes into a rage, I see the tree turn red as if it's saying, "Someone must pay with blood." That person who pays is not always the one to whom the bitterness is really directed. Did you ever take out your anger on your child when you were mad at your wife? People suffer from that tree.

The tree's fruit is in direct opposition to the tree of life, which produces the fruits of the spirit: love, joy, and peace. The bitter bush produces hatred, great sorrow, and confusion.

These demonic fruits often produce diseases, too. This is why many are sick among you; from this bloodsucking tree. This tree will even feast upon your blood, polluting it and the natural balance of the body. Then it will turn itself to the mind and cause depression and nervous anxiety. Bitterness is usually the underlying condition in mentally ill people. People suffer terribly from this silent killer, the worst of all sins. You can triumph over anything once bitterness is taken care of.

Do you have any of these fruits in your life in excess? Then look into your heart. Search your heart; let your mind remember what someone has done to you or even what you have done.

At first, the tree is just a small shoot. The shoot began from a small seed. That seed fell into rich soil, was watered, and finally burst forth into an unrighteous plant. It was a fast-growing tree, fed by the hurts and pains of life being stuffed inside and not dealt with. For many of you, it began as children. Things happened when you were so small, that they have been blocked out.

The tree's root system is intricate and goes deep, making it difficult to remove. That tree's roots look like claws as it holds tightly to its host. Yes, beloved, it is like a parasite, just like a dog carrying a dangerous tick on its neck. That dog can scratch and roll around, but once the terrible parasite is well imbedded, the poor animal will suffer, perhaps even die. So it is with you, little ones. For the tree of bitterness is a tree of death, living death.

You ask, "How do I get rid of this tree?" First you must understand the magnitude of it. Before a person starts to cut down a tree, he first looks at it and calculates how long it will take. The bigger the tree, the longer the chopping time. Then he picks up his ax and swings away. He begins to perspire and eventually, most people become tired. So, too, you must measure the tree inside you. Just how big is the bitterness inside you? How many times have you hurt others or yourself because of your pain? Search your heart. A good time to do this is when you are alone and relaxed. Thumb through the pages of your life.

Look at each chapter. How did it begin and end? There are seasons of life that are like standing at a crossroad. Standing at the crossroads, a person makes a life decision—that is, which way to go. My greatest desire is that you will choose the correct path. When you encounter your tree and begin the journey down through the chambers of your heart, it is so easy to become entangled in the thorns. That tree has many thorns that would ensnare you and which protect it from ultimate death. You will need My help to get down deep into the root. Simply ask Me to show you the root and seed of your bitterness. It may be very unexpected when I show you, for it's not always apparent. You may think you already know. Perhaps you think it's your spouse or boss, but it generally goes much deeper. Expect the unexpected. For some, it could be at birth or even before, in the womb. Then, after I have shown you the deepest root, ask Me to help you chop and dig it out, for it is like a cancer. Remember, when you get to the root, the tree with all its tentacles will die. Then, instead of trying to carry away all the cumbersome branches, trunk, and roots, ask for My Holy Spirit to light a cleansing fire in you to ignite the broken, withered tree. Ask for the cleansing fire from heaven to burn away the dross in you.

There is no greater sickness than bitterness. If you must be angry, be angry with the one who set you up for pain and destruction, the father of lies, the destroyer, Lucifer. I never ordain the destruction of My little ones. Like an earthly father, I watch My children make wrong decisions and then they pay sin's price—sorrow in one form or another. But I am the one who delivers you from Satan's wrath and from yourselves. And just like an earthly father, I pick you up, wash the sin's stench off you, and forgive and then help you. I never long to see you repeat the same mistake. Once the lesson is learned thoroughly, you need not relearn it. You have passed the test. Ask Me to shorten this whole process. Ask Me to send a Holy Ghost Chain Saw to make it easier and much quicker for the cutting of the wood and then the Cleanser's Fire. After the tree is cut and burned, pray for the Anointing Healing Balm of Gilead to flow into the cavern where the tree was and to heal the wound.

The root of bitterness actually sprung from the Tree of

the Knowledge of Good and Evil. For when Adam and Eve ate of its forbidden fruit, all manner of sin entered the human race. They were My test subjects, and sin was found in them in the deep places of their souls. Sin loves to hide in dark, dank places. It will always try to hide itself. Just as the root of bitterness, it goes very deep so it can hide.

Many of you do not appear to be bitter. You put on happy faces and try to hide your pain, but I see it. You even try to hide it from yourselves. This is dangerous and unnecessary. I don't want you to suffer. When you hide things, there is suffering, but when you face yourself, your past, and admit your sins, they can be cleansed whiter than snow. The tree of bitterness is so mean and unjust. It never belongs in My precious children. You do not need to carry its heavy load. Remember, a man named Jesus carried a bitter tree on His wounded back so that you would not have to carry a tree inside you.

Being delivered from bitterness is a process because it goes so deep. Forgiveness can take time. Occasionally, I do a miracle; "I do it quickly," but usually it takes time. It's like a surgery. And ultimately, the Great Surgeon is the one who does the cutting away.

You need only be willing to be honest with Me and yourself. You can be delivered, and I long to do it for you, dear ones.

DAUGHTER, I WANT TO TELL YOU ABOUT THE CROWNS ...

of glory. When a man has completed his course on the earth and comes to heaven, a crown awaits him. The crown can be gold, white, silver, scarlet or blue—gold being the highest award a person can receive. The reward is for great feats in the spirit: self-sacrifice, perfect love, a giving, loving spirit. These are what I cherish. They are the Jesus-Spirit personified. These are My high callings in the schools of life. The gold crown is for man, perfected and matured, completed by Me on the earth. Many men will not attain this crown because they won't let Me work these things in them. But those who do have a joy unspeakable awaiting them.

The silver crown is for those who have tried to walk in obedience and self-sacrifice, but whose flesh has been in their way some of the time. And the scarlet crown is for the ones who have been flesh-ruled, those who will make it into heaven by other's prayers—by the skin of their teeth and by My sovereign grace. These are the ones I have taken pity upon and will receive. I want all My children to receive the crown of perfection—the gold one. I don't like to give inferior gifts; I desire so much to give the best of everything. These crowns, the heavenly crowns, are called glory crowns. The crown of life is a crown that attaches itself to the head and melds with a man's spirit (in heaven). It is a crown of all heaven; it is life, life in all aspects—glorious, abundant life. It infuses the spirit of man with the wine of joy and gladness that stirs the spirit. This crown is a permanent putting on of heavenly qualities. There is an anointing crown also that I give to My angels (place into their hands). They then take this crown down to the earth and place it on a man's head, the man whom I have chosen for a job that I want done on the earth. As they place it on, there is great joy and a lovely ceremony. I do this sometimes while a man sleeps. This is part of how I teach a man while he sleeps upon his bed. When the anointing is placed upon a man, it's a package. In the package are all the things a man needs to know to do his job: wisdom, knowledge of his job or ministry; in other words, teaching on the subject. This is a sweet crown. It brings Me much joy to give this crown to a man or woman.

There is also a crown of sorrow. Jesus wore this one. It is the essence of selflessness. It is the crown that says a man is blessed when He lays down His life for a friend, whether it be physical death or a putting away of the flesh, in service to another. It is the intercessor's crown. It is also a joyous crown. Yes, there's sorrow in seeing what has happened to My creation, but the joy comes in breaking the chains of the oppression of My people through the giving up of yourself. There is also a crown of joy. This is the one I place on the head of man as a blessing for obedience. This one is so lovely. Joy is not just laughter and frolicking; it is the very essence of peace and strength.

There are crowns of obedience. In the face of great battle, when My children are faithful to Me and do as I say, they shall wear this crown. There is the martyr's crown for those who have died for Me. This is a special one that I give to only a few. This one is for those that "the earth was not worthy of," those who have been perfected in and through great afflictions, My sweet little ones, whom I love so.

Then there is a crown of righteousness. This one is given when a person overcomes an area of his life in which he has had troubles and temptation. My people can have many of these crowns. There's a crown of justice. This is the crown of the judge upon the earth. Very few of these have been given yet, but more will be given soon. These are for My people who will "judge the nations." When they speak, storm clouds will gather and pour rain at the pointing of their fingers. When they give the signal, a town will consume itself in fire. They will be as My warriors, they will do as I order them to do. There is a warrior's crown for those who will take cities and who will take people for Me. They shall do great battling in realms of the spirit and in the earth. They are the firebrands. They shall leap over walls and take cities!

There are numerous other crowns, but I won't go into these now. A man can wear many. Many people on earth have crowns stacked on their heads. They don't see them yet, but My angels do. One day soon, I will open My children's eyes completely to the Spirit world so that My children will go in and out of "two worlds." You will love it and be so completed. You will see what I do and then do it—just as Jesus did. Hence the scripture, "You walk in heavenly places." And, "As He is, so are you." As My Son is, so shall you be. Soon I shall unfold the holy pages of My Book, unwrap it as a great golden scroll with deep, strange, and lovely revealings unto man that man might be taken into My Word and literally become a part of it. I will unwrap and open man's heart to receive the revelation of My Word into himself. Man has only tasted a tiny scope of My Word because man has read it with a human, imperfect mind. But when I reveal it to a perfected, undivided mind and spirit, man shall soar through heavenly places. There is so much more, so much more than man's finite mind can fathom in My Scrolls. I have set planets and galaxies in motion by My Word. It can set things literally on fire. It burns with power. And soon, man shall behold this power.

DAUGHTER, YOU MUST NOT WORRY ABOUT MAN ...

and what he will say about you and how he will judge you when I give you words to write that don't fit into his neat "little theology." For man is man, but I am the Alpha and Omega, the ruler and reigner of all the universes and realms of the Spirit. I created all things. And as much as I love mankind, I must tell you that man is ignorant. Because man chose death, cursing instead of blessing, he fell from the grace and knowledge that I wanted to share down through the ages to come. I had many beautiful and exciting things to share with people. I wanted man to rely on Me for the knowledge and wisdom of "Your God." I did not want to see My children locked into a quiet, stupid stupor, unable to think and feel—like animals. I wanted to elevate man to a place where I could trust him with caring for universes. I wanted to bring him to a place where he would not exist without Me, but where I could trust him implicitly, where he could be trusted with My creation even beyond planet Earth. Alas, man failed, but I had a backup plan, and I still mean for My original plan to succeed.

Now let Me tell you the "Secret of the Snow." Write what I tell you with no thought for the puny mind of man, even your own. You may not understand all I tell you or even be able to truly believe it all now, but I will expand your mind to understand things I will tell you later.

In heaven there is a "Sea of Glass." A Crystal Sea. Satan has taken My most beautiful creations and made counterfeits, then scared people away from those things that are the most glorious of My creation, things I've longed to share with you. I long to share them with people through this prophetess. I do not have time to sugar-coat or coddle men and women when I tell you things about the workings of the Spirit Realm.

Some of you will not understand what I tell you and will become afraid, but don't let the enemy deceive you. If you judge My prophet, you will reap what you sow. Your own judgment will be used to judge you. It will be so with all of My anointed ones. Be wise, then, as serpents and as gentle and sweet as doves. My anointed ones have reaped hard pain through their lives that many of you cannot understand. You have all had a measure of pain, but there are those who have walked in places in the Spirit, who have reaped special assaults from the enemy that many of you cannot even imagine. I tell you these things, these nuggets, to open up new realms of the Spirit to you, to show you new universes because I love you. I have used an instrument made of flesh to write some of these things. Do not blame the instrument because she is putty in My hands. Pray that I will be able to expand and open your spirits and minds. These things that I long to share with you are not, after all, the deep, deep things of the kingdom, for you could not handle them. Your finite minds, your old wineskins, cannot yet handle the sweet "new wine" I shall eventually pour into them, for they would burst from the new effervescence of it. The new wine will have an intoxicatingly beautiful effect upon your spirits. The Song of Solomon says, "I have drunk my milk with my wine, and Thy love is better than wine."

You see, even My prophetess has been limited in what and how I would show her things to come. She could hold more than these truths I show you, but for you, I have had to soften truth for a baby who cannot handle meat yet. Lest you think she is elevating herself, do not believe it. She is just a person like you, but I have given her a God-given capacity to understand Spirit truths, just as you all have been given gifts. She, too, is still in infant stages of learning, so do not become jealous for she, too, is a human like you and she has paid dearly for the knowledge I have poured out on her.

Now about the snow. There is a "Sea of Crystal" before the throne of God, "A Glassy Sea." The sea burns continually with Holy Fire. Colors shoot out from it like a rainbow of beauty. Have you not seen water when it mixes with oil on pavement and seen lovely hues of color? In the colors of the Sea of Glass, there are new sights you haven't seen before, new colors of greater beauty than you have ever experienced: crystalline prisms, pure, Holy, and altogether a lovely reflection of My throne and Myself. I sit upon many waters. My throne is magnified upon many crystal waters, Holy waters. There is a hush over heaven, and then the boom of the thunder of My Holy voice is heard upon the waters, My voice that echoes down through the ages and into future ages. For in glory and majesty, My voice and My Spirit are upon the Crystal Waters. The angels and many peoples bow and fall prostrate upon their faces before Me, casting their crowns before "His Majesty," crying "Holy, Holy, Holy is our God, our God reigns forever and ever, Amen." My Voice is the voice of thunder and My Voice is the voice of many waters. For I Am in the waters and they in

Me. My Holy Spirit is in the waters and the waters in My Spirit. The "Secret of the Snow" is that as those waters flow and swirl in pristine and prismic beauty, a portion of them fall to earth down through galaxies, down through the Aurora Borealis and into the outer atmosphere of earth, where the coldness of the spirit that surrounds earth from the enemy's workers and workings hardens the waters in the darkness of space. But I make beauty of ashes. There, the waters become once again as crystal, a changed form. You say, "How could water come from crystal?" Didn't Moses get water from a rock? When the waters freeze, My hand creates each tiny drop to become a beautiful crystalline flake, each different, yet similar, like peoples of earth. All look alike when seen from a distance, yet under a microscope, each is different. Each one, like man, is able to diffuse light. Each one is able to radiate light in beautiful hues of My Spirit. As a hush falls upon earth, as around the Crystal Sea, the purity of My love falls upon a world that does not, for the most part, perceive Me or My limitless love. In the holy hush of falling delicate snow, I magnify My love for man and renew My covenant never to flood the world again and bring death in the form of water again. The next time of judgment shall be not water, but fire. But, I would that man would be saved from it.

Now, as the snow falls to earth from the heavens, the grass of the field dies. All this in due season. The snow brings temporary death, but only for a season. Then, when spring's warmth breaks forth, newness springs to life. Meadow flowers pop up and open to the warmth of the sun. Green grass fills the valleys, and life begins again. This illustrates My Kingdom's principles of renewal and new life. Even in the death of selfishness, there is new abundance of life born out of dead works. For listen, children: Under the blanket of temporary death, new beauty and hope and new situations abound—new birthings, born out of My Mind, for your good, fresh hope. I know you are in a time when it is easy to despair. Life seems stagnant and polluted, hard and harsh. But as the days become even darker, I will become lighter and brighter—a bright light in a dark world. You, too, will become brighter so that you can be light to a darkened, dying world. You must become the snow, gently falling, bringing death to old ways (old religious ways, old sins) and life to a sin-sick world. You will be misunderstood by many, but take no thought for this. My Son was not accepted by many. Remember, I accept you and I long to share with you My secrets that I have hidden so long from the world and religious man. You will need double knowledge and anointings and knowing Me in the days ahead. Revelations, which seem just beautiful bits of knowledge, will become steel in your hand in the days ahead. For I wish to take you above the lowly things that will shortly come upon Earth and into new heights of the Spirit and safety with Me. Your God reigns above the temporary cloud about to come upon Earth. Your God rules and reigns above all gods. Your God reigns above all the earth.

IN MY FATHER'S HOUSE ARE MANY MANSIONS ...

or places. Each of these chambers has qualities of its own. These mansions exist on earth as well as in heaven. They are portals, or places of dwelling, for My people. They are segments of being, with wondrous qualities of life existing in them. One of these places, or realms, is "The Garden."

Eden was a beautiful place of peace and serenity. It was protected on all sides by My Spirit Angels. No one was allowed to enter or leave except by My consent. It was cut off from the rest of the earth because fierce peoples roamed the world who had nothing to do with My Spirit. They lived in caves as animals. They were barbaric and wicked, and the earth was a torn place. Rumblings and thunders and storms wracked the planet. Demons worked havoc, and there was dark oppression.

But in the midst of the tempest was a place of repose, the lovely garden. In it, I set a man named Adam. He was My son and how I loved him. I could not find a wife in the earth wonderful enough for him, and so I created with My Spirit a lovely creature, the mother of creation, Eve. They were two lovebirds, two cooing doves, for the love I created between them was a sweet and precious incense to My nostrils. It was so good and lovely in the garden. Theirs was paradise. Their time was spent in contemplating the earth-shattering, mind-bending beauties there. They walked in cool, green jungles and picked luscious, dripping fruits and bit into them and were refreshed by their wonderful tastes and spirit-refreshment. They lounged beside crystalline pools so clear they could see lovely, fiery-colored fish in waters below. They watched crashing waterfalls and giggled at the mist on their faces. They looked at mountain peaks so lovely with snow gently capping their summits. They breathed air that was clear and refreshing, laden with the smell of flowers. They swam in oceans that lulled them in the gentle arms of their waves.

My children were so very much alive. When they talked, they held each other in their hearts; their very souls touched and they touched Mine. When they kissed, their mouths were anointed with sweet savors, love flowed between their lips and hearts. And when they made love, heaven was moved with the loveliness of two spirits becoming one with Me. In My grandest gesture two humans could express, there was such joy, satisfaction, and completion, that I was moved by the tenderness of it. They were My darlings. Oh, how I adored them and how completely it broke My heart to see their fall. They were My test of man's obedience, and they failed My test of love. I loved them so completely, so totally, that I gave them Myself. When we communed in the garden, heaven's portals and windows opened up to them. They saw Me and I saw them. And, oh, what wonderful times We had together. They were pulled into the Spirit Realm to dance the dance of lovers. We danced on the wings of the wind. There was spirit travel to the heavens and galaxies and so much more! There were times when the two literally became one and were taken supernaturally into Me. We were a family—the three of us. We had so much joy, it was indescribable. There was Spirit playtime, where we played games and laughed and love was always underlying everything.

There was always the knowledge that we were one and we were a family. It was so very good, and I wasn't lonely anymore. They would have had a large family to populate the earth. There would have been wonderful times with the children and grandchildren, more beautiful than words can describe; one big, happy, joyous, spirit-enlightened family. The earth would have been taken for Me, and total joy would have reigned. The oil and wine vats would have overflowed and the earth run with milk and honey; prosperity, peace, and joy and not an ounce of boredom. There would have been new pleasures and thrilling delights every moment and I would constantly have created more. But, alas, you know the story of disobedience. For it's been your story, too, but the days are late. Heaven's close for many. My chosen ones have endured much. I long to now have you enter My rest and a new Garden of Eden. This one will be different. It will have to be in the Spirit Realm for the earth cannot be transformed yet. But in this new garden, pleasures and refreshments abound. You do walk in heavenly places. You know the way. I am the way. Pray to go through the door into this realm. Pray to enter the garden. Pray to enter into the delights of the Spirit where all manner of sweet fruits abound. There you can drink deeply from deep caverns of crystal waters. In the waters, you will be refreshed. In the cool of the deep blue waters, My Spirit resides. In the lofty mountains, My Spirit resides. For I am in the mountains. In the mountains of spices, I Am that I Am. The way is narrow into the garden, and few shall find it, but, oh, those who do! There's joy there, and peace.

Ask Me and I'll lead you into the heights of My Holy Hill where your souls may find perfect peace and joy. It's cool and refreshing in the garden in the midst of a dirty and hot world. It's safe there for My children. Lie down there and sleep and awaken refreshed. Nothing can harm My children there. My little ones are tired and torn, but in the shade and coolness of the garden there is rest and peace. Joys and pleasures abound there for you.

Prophecy is the Spirit of refreshing and the Spirit of revival. You shall be the lifter of the heads of the brethren after your "Garden Experience" because you will have it in abundance to give to them.

THE CREATIVE WORD ...

works by the creative mind (the expanded mind), which works by the creative force in the Creator. When the hippies locked into some of the secrets of the universe (the expanded mind), their vehicle was a dirtied Satanical one—drugs, and though they saw some partial truths of God, which were, by the way, true (unity of brothers: non-Christian and Christian, separate, and all things being fused with one another in the universe), they were only partial, not absolute, truths. These are the days of quickening (making fast and alive) by God's Spirit. A particle in an oyster makes many small ripples (just as a coil in coffee water makes it boil and ripple). The light goes out from My Fingers (God's) and electrifies and soars through the universe and into the oyster's shell and quickens layers of sand to speed up, thus making a pearl. This works by the creative force of God, which is light. It is more than light (power), but for the simplicity of man's mind, I used that word to describe My power.

Faith is ruled and governed by love. The more perfect the love, the greater the faith and the greater the results.

The pearl of faith is in a protective shell of hope. Inside the shell is a lining that protects from germs, and the power or love (they are synonymous) of God reaches down and quickens the sand to become a pearl. Pearls, as faith, are rare, exquisite, and have varied values.

Hope in the heart shields faith, and love (or God's power) begins the process. When I say you will be walking in a "new" power, or "energy," of God, it is a new love of God—fresh and accelerated. This is how the revival will work: a new love anointing. Remember, hope in the heart shields faith and is quickened by love. It is a law, or formula, of mine. The pearl in the shell is in an ocean. The ocean is My Spirit and also life. There are tides to life, too. There are tides to My Spirit, also, hence, waves of glory. Glory is love power in action. Power is love. If you want to "tap into" the power supply, you must tap into My "love power." The Spirit helps your infirmities. The Spirit is the "Ministry of Helps" I speak of in My Word. When I say from glory to glory, you are being changed, I mean love in action, My action, and My love are continually permeating your spirits. The love comes in waves, have you noticed, in jets or bursts of power. That is so you won't be overcome and die in your natural bodies. My love is so powerful, the waves of it pulsate throughout the universe like jet streams. My love is speeding up because of the shortness of time, as is evil. Jets and quickenings of love power are going harder and faster into the earth and into men's hearts. This is where the birthing is being accomplished in fertile hearts. There shall be a new conception that "religious" man will not conceive because he is unable to conceive the Wind of My Spirit. The natural man will not comprehend the Spirit's life. The song, "The Cleansing Stream I see, I see, it cleanses, oh, it cleanses me" was written by a person who had a taste of things to come. In the jets of love power, healing will naturally come, because My love encases healing over diseases and healing of hearts. Jet streams are in preparation. New manifestations are ready to be powered through eternity and into the world of men. There will be angelic guardians and onlookers who will watch the panorama of love and glory. Man is soon to see the greatest display of My love power since the cross. Rejoice! The 4th of July and New Year's Eve wrapped into one are ready and about to be birthed. The day of redemption is close at hand. Rejoice!

When you put out your hand, that is hope. You say, "Let there be bread." That's faith and God's love power shoots through the universe and makes the faith take life.

Here's how we work it: "In heaven, when you just have a thought, it happens." You need only imagine a garden and immediately you are in a lovely flowered garden. God says to have a vision and that His people perish for lack of a vision. When you hold out your hand (of hope) you then picture what you want (by faith). Picture yourself thin, for example, and then say, "Jesus" to lock it in or bring the love power shooting into your vision. There will come a time when you just have to merely think it and it will become automatic (when He'll just enter the situation automatically). The Bible says His Name is above all names. This is part of the way He creates what we have faith for.

Visualize what you need or want.

Put out a hand of hope.

Say or think "Jesus," and wheels are set in motion instantly.

(Such as healing: Scan your body in your mind and see organs come into perfection and light throughout—then lock it in).

When light or love power goes through a crystal (which is the Word or Jesus), it becomes a diffused rainbow of lovely color taking on the aspects of the Creator. It is varied, able to set things, literally, on fire; the light is intensified by the crystal. It is beautiful, powerful, varied, a reflection, and a refraction-changed. The light is God's love power shining through Jesus (the Word) and becomes a changed, stronger force.

When the veil rent in the temple, it symbolized that the curtain had been removed from the world's eyes and spirits and that God had been revealed to man in His deity and that we could now enter through the torn flesh of the Christ.

In these end days, faith is going to change. We will not have to work things up. We will have faith charged with glory and love power and it will be no problem. It will just work automatically for those who know the secrets of the Kingdom. There will be even greater things happening.

(I want to see the One who is love.)

"In the beginning was the Word. That is the word that unlocked things. And the Word was with God and the Word was God." The word in man's vocabulary is Jesus. And the Word is the first works of creation—the Word Jesus. His actual name unlocks situations. His new name is a secret to us now but there will be a new name in heaven.

His heavenly name that will do other fantastic things. His name locks in and sets the wheels of the Spirit and Universe in motion. We dare to hope, we speak or think our desire and set the process in motion by the name of Jesus, spoken or thought (which is the power zapping down). It will all become so automatic and simple. However, we must be purified before we have this process fully given to us.

(These are power processes, but I want to see the Power Source face to face.) Visualize your head (mind) being filled with light (glory, love, power) then move to your spirit (center of diaphragm) then bowels (of compassion) then front and back of head (emotions) then hand (healing and bestowing love on others) then feet (He says, how lovely are the feet of those who bring good news-salvation to others) then loins (loins girth about with truth). Sex organs (reproducing). Your face magnifying the beauty and love of Christ (like a prism or crystal). Then Jesus will lock it in and bring it to pass. This process can change universes and move mountains.

When you speak to the mountain (the name above all names) the mountain will be cast into the sea. The mountain is our situations or others in their lives. You have enough hope to think about the mountain, then faith enters automatically, then love power enters and the situation obeys.

Faith process:

You have a situation.

Speak the Word (the Word is Jesus). The scriptures are merely to bring you to the place of being able to say Jesus.

Receive miracle.

Give God glory.

This tool makes Satan only a toy and nothing to be feared. We will just want to have speediness to travel around to defeat the foe in different parts of the earth (and it'll be so easy and automatic); instantaneous, quick and sharper than a two-edged sword—able to divide asunder between the marrow and the bone. The marrow is where things (blood or life) are produced. The bone is the completed thing. The Word is Jesus and He can cut between or change the production of situations and their completed form.

DAUGHTER, DO YOU REMEMBER ...

when you forgot to put your car into gear and it gently rolled back into an older man's car as you watched in horror? You braced yourself for the inevitable anger and loud harsh words that you expected to hear as you dejectedly walked toward the gentleman. But no, this gracious man said, "I'm so sorry that this happened to you. Is your car all right?" You walked away in disbelief as the kind man apologized over and over to you. Remember how you felt convicted, wondering if you would have been as gracious. That man's reaction was the essence of My character—sweetness and charity even toward those who make mistakes. Remember how the tears welled up in your eyes as you continued to ponder his kindness to you all the time that you drove home? Remember the disbelief?

That was because so few are kind these days upon your earth. There are still kind people, but their numbers diminish daily. There will be a day soon when the only truly kind people will be My own.

You see, people want their rights, their just desserts, what is coming to them. People have "their opinion." They are opinionated. People have become spoiled, arrogant, rude, haughty, high-lookers, their noses high in the air. This is not just among the well-educated, wealthier upper classes. The poor and uneducated also want to be heard. Someday, sit and listen to a talk show on T.V. Observe the attitudes of people's hearts. Are they gentle and humble, trying to find something to agree upon—peacemakers? No, they all have strong opinions; they have "their rights" and no one will change their minds. Theirs is a stubborn mindset. They are justified and no one had better step on their toes.

Compare this attitude to My Son's. He came to earth not to condemn mankind (which He had every right to do because of the great and horrible stench of sin that drifts up into the heavens). No, He came to earth in sweet humility to claim what was lost—man. He didn't come as a haughty king to receive the glory that really was due Him. He came to receive wounds, betrayal, mockings, and the ultimate horror and rejection—being hung by His sweet hands and feet on a tree. Then, even worse yet, he was taken to the place where ghouls reside, to taste of Hell's worst atrocity—separation from Me. The greatest aspect of My Son's total sacrifice was that He truly believed that with all the sins of the whole world laid upon Him, that I could never receive Him back into heaven with Me. For He loved you so that He was willing to go to Hell forever!! My Son was wounded, bruised, and even mutated in His natural body, not even looking human. From so much torture and sin laid upon Him, He truly did not resemble a human being. This may sound like a fairy tale, but believe Me, it was real. It happened!! Calvary was the "Atrocity of the Ages."

So I must ask you, do you have the right to judge another, even a sinner? Do you have the right to be anything but kind, gentle, and humble, even to those who don't deserve love?

I am watching you. I see the way you act toward others. I am hurt when you are small and petty. But I am so proud when you overcome natural human feelings and choose kindness instead of arrogance. I am overcome with joy when you choose the right instead of the wrong. Yet I do not condemn even when you do wrong. I am not a condemner, but a lover of man's soul. I am the lover of your soul!

Love one another as I have loved you.

UNTO YOU THIS DAY...

shall a strong word be given. You that sit in ivory palaces must come out; come out and listen to the "Words of the Lawgiver" and the "Lover of your souls."

From the beginning I created My children to be Mine, wholly, to be all and all Mine. But My creation had to be tried to see where their hearts lay. My lovely children failed the test. My Heart ached from loneliness before My created humans walked the earth. I found fulfillment in man, and then My heart was broken again. For man rejected Me by his tasting of sin. For the first sin was conceived, which was really the sin of witchcraft (placing another god over the true God). For then man made the fruit and the "deceiver" to be his god at the moment of the first bite.

And out of "a bite" came trillions upon trillions of bites of different fruits. And with each bite of each fruit, man has been stolen from, though he has thought he was the one doing the stealing or sinning. The enemy has subtlely (just as in the garden) placed sin in man's heart through sneaky, devious ways. Man has been a pawn in the hands of evil spirits. Man has been used. And I have had to watch the panorama of sin, the parade of it, from heaven. As My children marched by, bent on sin, I have had to endure the pain of it much more than them. Because I have seen the big picture, the unmasked ugliness, the horror of a world in the self-destructing throes of death. People have truly thrown away their lives and their babies' lives in the ultimate sin, that of witchcraft, of turning away from Me. I have sorrowed beyond what the human mind could conceive. You may think these things have been what only the world has been guilty of, but no, the heartbreak that I must endure is that My very own children have done horrible sins, too. After all, didn't My own children sin in the garden? Didn't My Adam, My gentle, kind, loving Adam and My sweet, sweet-hearted Eve turn from the One who loved them so tenderly to another god? Sin conceived brought forth the death of so many sweet darling children of Mine. So I had to take My precious little adorable Lamb, so lovely, so kind, so very good, a man that men could never begin to imagine the goodness and gentleness of. I had to let Him be slaughtered that you might live—so that you might be able to love and not lose your babies like I had to do the day My Boy was given for you. For on the day He left Heaven, My Heart broke, for My very life in Him was being drawn from My Own Spirit. I was split apart. I was emptied. I was again alone, for you!

When My precious Lamb, My Holy Son, was taken from My Father's bosom Heart, I had to learn again to be alone. My creation was almost dead to Me and My Son was gone. Much that I loved was taken from Me and I was brokenhearted. But, because I can feel so much more acutely than you, you cannot begin to know the pain. Have any of you ever lost a child or a person who was your life? Then you have had a taste of what I felt. But even in the pain, there was a joy being birthed and that was to know My children were coming home by the grace of the Son. So for the love of many, WE died upon a lonely hill. Yes, I was there, too, and I died a little inside when I saw My Child die; and I had to turn My back on Him and watch Him be escorted by horrible creatures in hellish flames.

But children, the story doesn't end here, for on the third day He rose from the land of the dead and into My arms! And when We met, Our Spirits were one again! The joy, the glory, the tears to have My Beloved again in His Father's arms and to have My sons on the earth back in their Father's arms, to have a way back to heaven to the Father and the Spirit and the Son … to their family!

But children, you have strayed away and left Me so many times. Each time you sin, you leave Me; then I restore you; then you leave again only to return. But it cannot always be, for the world grows darker each day and the light is waning. Soon there will be twilight, then full darkness. "The sun and the moon will lose their light. Gross darkness shall cover the earth." This will not just be in the Spirit and in the earth, but the darkness in men's hearts will become so great, their witchcrafts will become so horrendous, that even the earth will be in physical darkness. My people, who are called by My name, will then become such great lights that their very presence will be the light that lights planet Earth. Their saltiness will be the seasoning that will salt the earth. For even the oceans shall dry and lose their saltiness. And if My people humble themselves and pray and turn from their wicked ways, I will hear from heaven and heal their land. I don't mean America's land or Russia's land; I mean the land or the spiritual property of My people. I will heal My people's spirits, souls, and bodies. It will please Me so greatly to see My creation again being Mine.

But in order to do this, My people must be cleansed and judged. My people have been through Gethsemane. They have chosen life or death, blessing or cursing. Now must come the cross. It hurts Me to have to put My children upon the cross of the death of self because I know the pain, but it pleases Me, too, because I know the victory. It will be the ultimate victory. When the swords in spirit clash between the enemy of your souls and My angel warriors, you shall come out of the battle strong and mighty, an army of My children who will take planet Earth back for Me.

It will be worth the judgment. It will hurt us both, but it will be worth it. When you have become like Me with no grossness to hinder you, then your light shall break forth as the morning. I have not been able to be close to man because of sin. My Son has always had to stand between you and I, the Father. How I've longed for My children, My babies. When the terrible stain of sin is removed from you, then We can meet face to face. Then Jesus, the mediator, can become Jesus, the Brother, and you can become an equal brother in all ways, an equal heir with Christ. I can then be the trusting Father I've always wanted to be, for you will be worthy of My trust.

Let not your hearts be troubled, neither be afraid, but trust in Me. Know that though the path is narrow and straight, I am on the path to help you. Know that I loved you enough to prepare a place for you; that where I am, you might be also.

Know that I care enough to judge you. For if I didn't, We could never be together in the Holy Place. Know that after a little while, you will come up into My Holy Hill with a pure heart.

Heed the words of the prophet for they were written with a great price.

Remember the joy of the Lord is your strength. For even in judgment, there shall be joy. For as you are washed from bloodstained, blood-guilty garments, you shall be white as snow.

I saw a white tree with almost all its branches cut off and the ones that remained (only two or three), those few remaining branches were the overcomers, those who will remain till the end. The leaves upon the branches were the works done by them.

DAUGHTER, TRUE HUMILITY ...

is knowing who you are and who Jesus is. My Son, Jesus, was a man who never tried to attract attention to Himself. He was not self-centered, but God-centered. He did not consider His own hurts, but those of others, even those who hurt Him. He was a lovely, completely beautiful person. He was gentle and tenderhearted. He was sensitive to others. He had great compassion for people. He committed Himself to others. Though many shunned Him, and some used Him, He still gave freely of Himself.

Do you know that everyone has to be submitted to another? Even I, the Father, am. When I made covenants and promises to man, I submitted Myself. I said I'd have to destroy Myself if I broke them. I was submitting Myself to the promises and to man. It's a spiritual principle; we all must serve each other. That's the way it is in heaven—The Golden Rule.

Humility is a wonderful quality. It makes life new and wonderful. It's like looking through a child's eyes. The world becomes new, when you're truly humble. Being humble is being willing to try new things, being pliable and not stubborn. Pride was born out of unworthiness, fear, jealousy and the need for attention. Satan, is the father of this dread disease; pride. Pride is anti-God and anti-goodness. Pride really does go before a fall. It has its own built in fall. When man walks in a spirit of pride, he is walking toward a precipice. He deludes himself with his bloated self-image.

If man could view himself and then Jesus, he'd be embarrassed and so painfully aware of his own rebellious, dirty heart; that's why My Son and I have spared man. We have not wanted to belittle our children; we just want everyone and everything to be joyous. Man is the one who makes his own ugliness. Man is bewildered. Mankind doesn't even know where he is going. Without My Son and Me, mankind would have self-destructed long ago. We have kept the human race from falling. People need Jesus and me. We love people and want Our family to be near us too.

Many people look at others, the retarded, derelicts, the poor and prostitutes, and feel self-righteous and a bit better than those less fortunate. They practice the cast-system in America too. There is a social cast-system even among many nationalities I've created. This should not be. These people need help. Many of them were not born lazy and dirty, just without a real chance in life. They need someone to encourage them and pray for them.

Humility and worthlessness are not to be confused. Humble people know they are someone because they were born of a royal spirit. They are kingly servants. They are gentle and sweet. Love and humility go hand and hand.

Arrogance and pride are so unworthy of My children. These should be the most foreign things in the world to My little ones.

Meekness and quiet gentle Spirits are what I treasure. You needn't puff up yourselves or make yourselves look important. For when you humble yourselves and make yourselves of no account, I'll raise you up into glory. You will be worthy to be honored.

SECTION 5

THE JACKAL IS AT THE DOOR

He believes he can open it and destroy whom he chooses, but on the other side of the door is the "Lion from the Tribe of Judah." I am a "fierce lion," who will protect MY young. Just let My cubs nuzzle under My chin and belly where there is protection from the jackal. Underneath My body there is warmth, peace, quiet, and protection from stormy days. Underneath are the everlasting arms, arms of fortified steel that cannot be broken or beaten. Nothing is strong enough to move My arms that hold My little cubs. Dark days are fast closing upon the world, but when darkness comes, don't animals hibernate and rest in peace? When snows create dangers in the woods, the bears crawl into holes to relax and sleep, hardly noticing the cold and treacherous blizzards. Even if a reptile crawled in with the bear, they would rest together in peace.

The bear, protected in a furry cocoon, would awaken to birds singing and sunshine, a new day.

Crawl into My arms. Trust Me to take care of you. I will. I've made a way. When the wolf is at the door, your hero is, too. "Superman" is just waiting to avenge that parasite. I will raise My children up as supermen and superwomen, too, by osmosis. By resting in My strength, they shall take on My super, mighty qualities. The way is prepared. Walk therein. Be not afraid of the pestilence or plague that walk at noonday. Be not dismayed. The birth pains must be felt in earth that My "sons and daughters of light" can be brought into their holy ministries. Be not afraid of what man or beast can do, just know that I will overcome and repay.

I DO NOT FIND PLEASURE ...

in seeing people fall. I made each person. I breathed life into them. I watched them when they were children. I hovered over My creation, brooding as a hen. Does a hen leave

her chicks? No! A chick may leave or become separated
from its mother, but she doesn't desert it. I want you to
know ... I love man. I repeat ... I love man. I hate sin, not
the sinner. Even in My wrath to come, I'll never forget
mercy. Even though it may look as though I have, I never
will turn away a repentant man. I died that the whole world
could be saved, not an elect group. However, some will
strive with Me to their own destruction. Their rebelliousness will cause their own suffering and eventually, spiritual
and physical death.

So children, when you speak of judgment, in your wrath,
remember mercy. For My wrath that shall be poured upon
the nations shall come partly from the lips of My children.
But, I also want you to remember mercy. For I am gentle
and lowly, as well as strong in battle. I am a gentle warrior.

I LOVE YOU, OH DAUGHTER

My ways are not your ways. The fiery sky at midnight
and buildings burning; these things you will see. But, I tell
you again, you will have peace. This is hard for you to
believe or understand, but it will be "My peace," and not
your own. It will not be a faith-kind of peace, but "God-
given peace," directly from Me. You will not have to try to
be peaceful, you just will be. I am a carpenter, building precept upon precept. These things must come to pass before
the Son of Man comes again. And, oh, the glory of that hour,
you can never even imagine. Nothing you will ever go
through in this life will even be remembered or considered
important when that moment comes. It will be as though
scales were falling from your eyes and you will see. My
thoughts, My deepest thoughts, will become known to you.
Oh, daughter, the glory of that hour excites even Me. I long
for it. I've waited patiently for it for 2000 years. For you
truly are the fruit of My womb.

When you hear the trumpet blow and see your true love

in the sky and He brings you to Him, oh, the joy for us all will be complete! I'm so excited that I can hardly wait! My children are coming home! My loved ones are coming home to Me, their Father! You can never imagine what joy there is in this for Me!

So when you see the unpleasantness start, rejoice, because it will mean the time is very short. And please, do not be afraid. I won't let you down. If I say you will have peace, you will. In fact, there will be such excitement in seeing prophecies fulfilled that you will forget to be afraid. These days of horrors to the world will be cut short and they will not be a horror to you, but a confirmation. I say once again, do not pine and wail for this evil world, because I have given them and will give them every chance to come to Me. The ones who do not are tares. They are evil, so do not cry for them. They know perfectly well what they are doing. It is not so much that they do not believe in Me, but that they would not serve Me, no matter what I would give them in return. They love their wickedness. Intercede in prayer for people everywhere to be saved, for it is My will ... that the tares be separated quickly from the wheat.

I love you and all My children. When you cry, I am saddened just like a mother. When you are joyful, I am so glad. When you overcome, I am like a proud Father. I even brag to the angels and other saints about you, My wonderful children. I love you with such a love that you will never understand until We meet face-to-face and I can show you.

So, be of good cheer, for I have overcome the world. I am always with you. I will never forsake you. I listen joyfully to your prayers. I am always close to you, watching everything you do. I am your helper, companion, and friend. I am informal and want you to be informal with Me. Talk to Me as to a close friend. Listen for My voice, because I talk to you and sometimes you're too busy to hear or you think you're hearing your own words, but it's Me, knocking at the door of your heart. I would that you have life and life more abundantly. I am with you, My children. Feel My presence!

SET FREE, SET FREE!

Would you like to be set free from the chains that are around you in the Spirit Realm? You will be.

Great Satanical armies have been set against you because of the greatness of the day I have chosen for you and chosen you for. Once the great wheels of deliverance are set in motion, nothing can stop them. There is an appointed hour, a time of your destiny, that has been chosen that nothing can destroy, no angel or devil. Your life has had governors set upon it. You could only go so far because I knew if I let you, you would go far from Me. So I have had to hold you back as a bridled horse, as a fiery colt that needed taming. It has hurt you deeply, but it had to be done because of the glory of the last hour. This is not to say that I have set Satan to try to kill you or put the many ugly things into your life that he has. When he has tried to destroy your life, I have stopped him!

Now that time is short, I have brought you to a place where I can do new things in you and through you. The "colt" shall soon be set free. Oh, what a glorious freedom it will be for one who has been bridled by Me and chained by Satan for so long.

"Deep calls to deep at the sound of your waterfalls, all your waves and billows are gone over me." Remember the beauty and exhilaration you felt at Mount Rainier? Your thirsty, dry soul and spirit in the Spirit Realm reached out and drank of the beauty and refreshment of the pure white mountain and clear waterfalls you saw. You felt elated, refreshed, and joyous to be in high places, but when you really experience these concrete, real changes in your life, you shall be made whole in Me. Complete joy shall fill you and overflow to others. You shall infect others with pure, exhilarating, fresh hope and joy.

Wait, daughter. The hour is minutes away. Wait, daughter. It's just around the next bend.

DEAR SWEET DAUGHTER ...

again I say, I love you. I see what your days have been like. They shall not always be this way. When Satan comes to steal your peace, bind him. When your children will not mind and rebel, bind him. I will help you more and more each day. I want you to be consistently joyful. I know life has difficult moments, for I also walked among men. I know about temptation, too, because the devil tempted Me also. I know what it's like to cry and feel agony in My Spirit. But My agony was for the whole world. I know what it's like to deal with unkind people because I did throughout My ministry. But through the fires of your life, I've never left you. I've always been there. No matter how you behaved, I've always loved you. Through frustrations and fear, I've been with you. Through all the dangers and pain, I've been with you. I long to turn this toil of yours into joy, and I will. There are new exciting days ahead and you shall be part of the "new young breed." There are days ahead that will make you forget these days of suffering. I long to really open Myself up to you and I shall in My time. I shall be more a part of you than you can imagine.

You shall magnify Me and you will be amazed at yourself. You will hardly know yourself. And you will see what your Holy God can do. Also, I will perform on your children's behalf. And you will hardly recognize the change I shall wrought in them. For I love your children. One shall be a gentle, kind person with the harshness out of her spirit. And the other shall be a great spiritual witness for Me. Her cheerfulness shall cheer others all her days, and her gentle, kind, and sweet spirit shall change lives. One shall be to others a testimony for the Word's power; she shall raise people from the dead and be an inspiration of love to many. There is a real sweetness and a great love and loveliness in your precious little ones, but Satan has taken their beauty and tarnished it with rebelliousness and anger, but not forever. Your husband shall be a gentle, loving, wise father and husband, and you shall be amazed at him. He has those seeds in him right now, but they must blossom. His anger and lackings will be put down, and he shall shine among men.

I do these things, daughter, for you, because you have suffered and prayed and because I do desire to bless you much more than you know. Love your Father. I love you, lovely daughter.

THE DEATH OF PLANET EARTH IS AT HAND

The animals are dying. The forests and flowers are wilting and wasting away. The fish in the seas are caught in the throes of death. The very air you breathe is losing its life-giving properties. The ground you walk upon is losing its abilities to shoot forth tender buds and is cracked and parched from lack of water, as a dying man staggers from thirst in the desert. Oceans and rivers are drying up into dust bowls.

But the worst of all this is that man is dying. He's being killed in many forms. "Molech," the God of fire, is hungry for the blood of children. He has required a sacrifice of flesh, and that flesh is in the womb of woman. Saline is a burning fire to the child who dies in agony in the hidden, tender reaches of the inner parts of the mother. Many children are cut asunder and still others are "sucked from their sanctuaries." They come not into this world to taste of the sweetness and agony of life, but they enter this world, through death, at the hands of "smug murderers." These baby-slayers are controlled by money and their father;

Satan, the evil one. These people who kill the "innocents" for profit, shall sip, one day, of the Lake of Fire--the same fire that they have caused these precious children to drink.

If I sound cruel or hateful, don't believe it. I have shown man mercy for so much longer than any human being would ever have. Man is so incredibly wicked and growing remarkably more so with each day and each moment that passes. His heart is becoming more and more "inspired by devils" and ambassadors of the evil one. Thoughts are being put into the mind of man that are completely inspired by Satan. Wicked thoughts are being transported out of the depths of evil. Men are doing unthinkable things to children and women, things too evil for Me to tell you.

The innocents of the land are being torn apart. My heart breaks for My creation that was created for beauty, joy, and delight. I created the loveliness of nature, the gurgling and cooing of a sweet little baby, clean, white, snowy mountains, air that is so pure that it seems to be drunk more than breathed, pristine green, dewy valleys, gentle gurgling streams, and miles upon miles of wilderness untouched by man ... virgin, beautiful. These were My lovely gifts to you. The family living in peace on their land, raising bountiful gardens full of delicious food, sitting by the crackling fire at night, laughing and singing, and getting up to a fresh country breakfast to have another day together in joy; these things are almost gone now and shortly will be.

My earth is becoming a "habitation for owls and all manner of strange and forbidden creatures." There are geneticists who even now are playing God. They are altering life. They are crossing animals with My treasure, My joy, My created human beings. They will eventually create other species and races. The scientists are also playing with the plant life, changing what I have created to be perfect. They are playing with all of nature, even the air you breathe and the water that sustains you. They will not be satisfied until they have ruined My creation, for they, too, are inspired by devils. The devil is hungry and roars as a lion, thirsty for the blood of humans.

Sin in the earth is so thick that if you could see into the Spirit, you would see the earth covered as "a cloud of thick, clotted, putrefied blood." It is the blood of saints who have been and will be martyred in the end of time. It is also the blood that the Beast extracts from so much sin. I see the cloud hanging heavily over earth, pushing down more and more upon mankind. On one hand, it is the blood of innocence and on the other, the blood of death. I weep and mourn for My people, for Zion. I weep and mourn for the sinner who doesn't know I exist. My Son, Jesus, the intercessor, cries before My throne on the outer rim of heaven, at what is before His eyes. The Spirit mourns each day more and more for what is, and worse yet, for what is about to be. For even My children will die, those of Mine who are not strong enough in Me to survive. For weren't there "five wise and five foolish virgins" in the parable? Didn't five, that is half of them, not have enough oil (My Presence) to make it through to the "wedding of My Dear Son and His wedded bride?" Those five foolish Christians became desperate for oil. They knew they were lacking. Their lights (the light of their lives, namely My Spirit-Anointing) were going out. They were being blotted out, as the sun sinks in the western sky, first in a ball of fire, then into sudden darkness. In desperation, they sought to borrow from My "anointed ones" some of their "fire." They said, in essence, "Give me some anointing. Give me some fresh hope. Give me some new wine. Give me light! Give me knowledge of the truth, the One who is truth, give me faith and love. Give me what you have; give me the Bridegroom." But you see, they waited too long. They had not, in times past, wanted to suffer; they had mocked the gifts of the Spirit, thinking in their hearts that those who were filled with the Holy Spirit were a joke, that those who spoke with other tongues, in Heaven's language, were comical or pathetic.

They mocked the prophets and spurned the apostles of Christ. The evangelists and teachers became people to snicker about. But I will not be mocked. I am also a "Lion," not a pathetic, roaring, "devil-of-a-lion," but I Am The "Lion From The Tribe of Judah!" I am strong in battle. I am able to, with a breath from My nostrils, blow planet Earth and all its sin into the reaches of nothingness. With a thought, I could wipe out all traces of the earth and every human on it. But for the love of mankind, I do not breath a hurricane of devastation nor think of the destruction of all men. At one time, I did repent that I had created you, but not for long. For when I hear a baby cry, hear a child call her mother, "Mommy, mommy," see the gentle, tender embrace of a man caressing his sweet wife, or see a man helping his fallen brother, I repent of bringing evil upon My peoples of the earth. I am kind, merciful, gentle, and long for you all. I long to see men brought up from the pit dug by the enemy into a clean, joyous walk with Me. I love to see ugly situations in people's lives changed into beauty. I love to make "beauty from ashes." Ashes are what are left after fire. They are the end product of the "fire of sin." But just as I mixed spittle with dirt and rubbed it on the eyes of the blind man and he was able to see, so, too, I long to pour "My new wine," into the ashes of your lives. I desire to spread them upon your eyes with which you do not see (and are deceived) and watch you open your eyes to see the truth and be set free. I long to have free people in a world of bondage. You say, "Not possible. We could never even exist when there is mayhem and chaos on every side." That is not true. I am life!! The life is in My Son's Blood. You are My people of covenant. You are, so to speak, in a cocoon of blood, a covering of the precious spilled blood of the "Sacrificial Lamb."

No devil can enter the blood realm of My "Son." I can keep My children in this realm though the earth staggers and sways as "a drunkard," though death reigns on every front, though the earth is moved out of its place, and the mountains are moved in their places, though the stars fall from heaven, and boils cover humanity, I am there with you. Though you go into the depths of the sea or into the highest heavens, I am there. I will never leave you nor forsake you, little flock, for it is the Father's good pleasure to give you the keys to the kingdom.

SECTION 6

AMERICA IS FAT ...

fat on her gluttonies and drunkenness, fat on the blood of little children; and shortly, fat upon the blood of the infirm, the old, the Jews, and finally upon the blood of the saints. For surely America has put a silver goblet to her lips and drank deeply of great destruction to herself.

Americans who are always on diets will have a rude awakening, especially those who glutted themselves and then could not bear to look in the mirror because of their fatness (as so many skeletal people walk the earth). America will soon become a living skeleton herself. She will remember when her body was round and plump, how she had to fight "the bulge" and will lament for those days. She will remember, with great sorrow, the lovely dainties she craved and ate as she watched her "God," the T. V. She will be reminded of how she sat with a sandwich in one hand and a remote control in the other and switched channels because she could not bear to watch starving children in Africa, not that she ever was tempted to call and pledge any of her precious mammon to help someone else. No, it was too easy to "switch channels." Oh, America, how I grieve for you and your children, who will shortly become those "children in Africa." How unaccustomed you are in your comfort to the horrors that the rest of the world must endure. Alas, because you have spilled the blood in the womb, you shortly will have to pay with your own children's blood. You have martyred babies, and you will now pay with your own babies' lives. I will make this very clear to your nation— that when you kill or even condone killing, you reap what you have sown, and that is the death of your own family. For when you forget to show mercy to others, you are then judged with the same judgment you meted out! When all this happens, do not blame Me. Many tried to tell the people of America that abortion was evil.

America was warned, but her heart was stubborn. To those who will not hear truth and be set free, they shall become the children of bondage and slavery.

America the beautiful has become a filthy harlot and her filth is truly in her skirts. Her wickedness is her shame and truly, I tell you that other nations look at her even now and "wink." Still others turn their heads in shame as they blush. She has become a byword already, but shortly, she shall become a horrible name upon the tongues of foreigners as they watch in awestruck terror as the jewel of this world becomes blackened by the judgments with which America shall judge herself. For truly, I would not have to do anything to her, because the "Land of Purple Mountains' Majesty" shall become the land of "Red Mountains Horror." Sudden destruction shall overtake her as an abandoned woman, while running from holocaust, aborts her child.

For America, who was once My lovely land of plenty, shall become more and more a habitation for owls and all strange and evil creatures. I mean this truly, for the scientists are even now playing with the animals, crossing species and creating monsters in the laboratories.

Because of the filth of so much wickedness, and because she was so anointed by Me and then so utterly rejected Me, I shall turn her over to strange torments. Things never heard of before shall plague her people. Water shortages, unparalleled in history, shall create a bowl of dust, insects, mildews upon plants, incredible swarms of insects gone awry, oversized. Toxic chemicals shall seep up from the dry ground, poisoning plants, then animals, then humans. Up the biological chain, these horrible chemicals that are mixed with other chemicals shall come. They will become deadly. Even in their dry powdery forms, they shall infuse the lungs, burning men to death. Prehistoric animals, hidden in deep places, shall arise to terrorize humanity. Horrible weapons and bombs shall explode, killing innocent people and children; fire and brimstone shall be upon your planet. Mutated creature-like people shall roam in groups with terror written upon their foreheads.

Once a person is stamped and marked with 666, they will change from a normal person into a wicked entity. Even if they had seemed somewhat good-hearted, now they will become Satan's child, wholly taken over by demonic forces.

Tell My church these things shall come to pass. Tell My people. Many of My own sit in almost as much darkness as the world does.

Tell them to seek Me while there is still enough light that I can be found, for when the light goes out in the world, people will be stumbling and falling in the dark gloominess, and it will be too late. Tell them that persecutions have now begun in America and will shortly be stepped up just as a woman in the end stages and most painful part of labor. Tell My people not to fear, but to be wise as serpents while still being gentle as doves. I tell you, this: you cannot trust too many, for many shall cry: "Lord, Lord," and I'll say, "I knew you not, for you are the embodiments of Judas, the betrayer." Be wise, choose extremely carefully who you trust and befriend. Pray carefully about your acquaintances and friends, for they may be the ones who will deliver you up to the temple or church to be killed. Think of it. Many will be dragged away to be horribly murdered, not just in government buildings and the prison camps that are even now being prepared, but many will also perish in the churches. Many will be dragged, screaming, into the very churches where they attended Sunday school and listened to their pastors preach, and will, in front of many, be martyred for My sake. Satan shall truly "wear out" the saints as someone would grind a leather shoe into the street, making holes in it, and destroying it— leaving it lying in a heap. That is why I tell you to be smart, be wise, so that this is not your fate. For many wolves slink about dressed as sheep. They look the same, act the same, talk the religious talk, but their hearts are open graves, lurking and waiting as spiders for an innocent fly to get caught in their webs of deceit. They lie in wait for their victims. Money is their God, not I. They love flattery and deceit. Some are so deceived, even now, that they really believe they are sheep and wheat, not wolves and tares. This makes them even more dangerous. When a person is deceived and is also zealous, they can enter into a holy war and kill many. I warn, you; listen! Examine your own heart and ask Me, now, right now, to remove the destroyer from your inner man that sin will find no place in you. Judas would never have believed he would have betrayed Jesus. If anyone would have hinted at it, Judas would have become indignant. That is the clue to deception—self-protection.

Ask Me to remove the darkness from your spirit so that I can reside, unhindered, in you. Pray for M E R C Y; for evil days are fast upon you. Cry out to Me. Ask Me to help you to cry out, before destruction as the world has never seen falls upon your foul-land, putrid with innocent blood. Pray that the priests of Baal, whose hands drip with the blood of children (and soon shall launch into new segments of society to kill) turn to Me in repentance. For I would not even turn the worst of the worst away, even though in their one hand they hold knives and in the other, they clutch their mammon. I still grant them a little time to repent. But if they will not, they will sip My fiery venom that I have created for the evil murderers of earth. For theirs shall be a special death and Hell reserved for the devil's right-hand men.

Pray and cry aloud in great agony of spirit for what is about to be loosed upon you and your children, unless I take pity and spare you from the wickedness about to overtake your country and then your earth.

AMERICA, THE ONCE LOVELY ...

beautiful, righteous woman of the earth is quickly becoming the great whore of your planet. When other nations speak of her, many wink at her sinfulness. She is becoming a byword, and the word is "harlot." I speak of America in the feminine gender for many reasons. I wanted to protect this place as My wife, whom I had adorned with lovely beauty, and also because I wanted her to welcome suffering people to her shores, where she would open her arms widely to embrace them, as a mother. Because Israel rejected My Son, America was to receive not only her blessing, but also the anointing I had given to Israel. That anointing was to make disciples of all men. That great commission that fell upon America was effective for a time. There was a church on practically every street corner. Missionaries were sent to the ends of the earth. The power of Pentecost fell on Azusa Street. But then sin and compromise crept onto the shores of "America's heart." Evil men invaded, yes, secretly invaded her government! Corrupt leaders with evil agendas slunk into the rulership of your nation. Like serpents, they propagated and lured other unsuspecting, naïve, or sinful men into their schemes. America was doomed. America was doomed many years ago. Because none of her modern-day presidents would totally stand for righteousness, I could not heal the nation. Remember great men in the Bible who stood for goodness and righteousness, such as Abraham? They paid a price for it, but nevertheless, their houses survived and prospered. So it would have been with "the land of the free." If one president had stood against all odds, America could have been saved. But alas, men's hearts always lean toward sin. The human heart seems to be attracted to sin as a moth to a candle. If My Spirit did not dwell in the hearts of some men, the world would have consumed itself long ago. For only My Spirit, reigning in man's heart, can free him or a nation. Without the Holy Spirit prevailing in a land, there is bound to be "all Hell breaking loose"—literally.

Without My Spirit dominating a land and its people, abuse flourishes. Don't think that I do not keep "the night watch" over little, rosy-cheeked angels asleep in their beds. For to Me, they are little angels, innocent, precious darlings. I also watch as beastly men with no consciences go into these little ones and spoil them. These men, who are so taken over with animal, and yes, demonic lust, go into their little babies and hurt and use their tiny delicate bodies. They throw them around as if they were dolls ... disposable playthings. These brutal men hurt their little children physically, but the damage they do to these little one's souls is beyond comprehension. The soul of the abused victim, no matter what age they are, is chopped and splintered, torn asunder. The mind literally cracks and separates, leaving the victim open to even more demonic influences. As the skin on the hands becomes cracked and open, even in extreme cases, bleeding, so, too, does the soul and heart of man. The more they become damaged, the more vulnerable they are to continuing damage. Man has not really understood the far-reaching, all encompassing effects that abuse can have on a person, especially a person who is not immersed in My Spirit. Saint Paul was an example of that. Because he was older and very close to Me, he could weather abuse without becoming so wounded in the mind and heart that he was destroyed by it. Children and many adults, however, are not where Paul was in the Spirit Realm. Because of this, they are either destroyed completely by abuse or just barely "get by." Old generational curses are often the door through which Satan can enter and bring the spirit of abuse upon the victim. Then, because of ignorance about spiritual warfare, many are lost to this vicious crime. For truly there is a horrendous war going on. It is a war against those who are vulnerable, My little ones. It truly would be better if the men who harm them were to put a heavily weighted stone about their necks and cast themselves into the sea rather than hurt one of these little ones. It would be better for them to pluck out their eyes than to lust after and hurt them. For the abusers will have special places in Hell, just as they do in the jails of the earth. Even the inmates in prisons recognize this sin as being so despi- cable that they sometimes will rape or kill the abuser. Even though I am aflame over this predominating crime of abuse, I still have not forgotten mercy. If the abuser will come to Me for help, I will never, never turn him away. I will help him and be his Father if he will just come to Me for help. My main purpose is not to punish, but to forgive.

I would even heal your country, if your leaders would turn to Me, but they will not. They love money and pleasure more than Me. Because of this, strange, weird, unearthly things will come upon America. Things that go beyond man's imagination. America will become that place spoken of in My Word, full of unclean animals, a strange desert, full of owlish and bizarre creatures.

AN EVIL GENERATION ...

has laid hold of their idols of decay. I saw in a row idols that I once loved: a TV, a VCR, a beautiful outfit laid exquis- itely on a chair, a lovely ocean beach (a vacation), a table laden with gorgeously decorated foods, a quaint country cottage, and beautiful furniture—all things my flesh esteemed highly, and suddenly, out of the TV and VCR came ugly demons: the outfit was a dirty rag, the ocean beach was black, and soot rained like an atomic blast, the food molded, the cottage fell in a heap, the furniture disintegrat- ed, and all the money had blood on it. What was left was only the purity and truth of God. Without the things that had so muddied my pleasure-filled life, only God remained. You said, God, you would show me how selfish I am and how the motivations and desires in my life have been so self-centered. Do I not owe it to You to be God-centered in all that I do? Your Son never sought to esteem or satisfy Himself, but always to satisfy you and help others. This was the center of all He did. Should I do less? If my land I inherit and inhabit is to be barren of worldly things, is that too much to demand of myself? My flesh hates it, but my spirit loves it. You gave all. "The Great One of The Universe" gave all out of His unselfish and lovely Spirit. You never "had to" do what you did—just as I don't. But how ungracious and unthankful of me if I refuse. When I am left with nothingness, will I not have everything? Oh, to fly "on the wings of the wind," to know purity of spirit-truth ... YOU! You are all in all and I am next to nothing at all, except for your love. But your love has made me great! How precious that My Sweet One has made a worm of dust great. A worm becomes a butterfly. From insignificant to lovely and graceful ... created by the love of a creator, a worm charged and surged through with the purity of sweet love. The Father-creator ... lover of my soul has made me great. And I must in turn make Him great in my life. It's only fair that I return the favor—the favor of the Lord. Oh, that my heart would understand and not be deceived and could walk the way of the cross. Oh, grant me the ability and the perseverance to do Your will and to win the race and be accounted worthy. I pray with fear and trembling, working out my own salvation, that I would not miss the mark of the high calling of God.

AS I LOOK OUT UPON THE CURSED THING...

that was once the blessed America, I would faint except that two angels sustain me and hold me up.

America the beautiful has become America the abomination. She was once as a beautiful woman, the most lovely, the most blessed, arrayed in finery, the upright, regal queen of all the earth. Now, as I look upon her, she has become a leper, a harlot, fallen beneath the lowest of all gross and filthy women. For the sperm and blood of evil men was upon her skirts, and her belly seemed blown away, and there was no child left there. For she had strangled and cut the little one who had lived within her own body. Her filthy mouth leaked vomit, yet she still flirted and winked at the men who passed by, hoping for more gold and jewels. She was beyond deplorable, scarcely human anymore, yet she didn't know her condition and she did not know her end because she was so completely deceived and darkened.

The angels had to steady me, lest I had died from the sight before my eyes. In the streets, wild animals ran about frantically. There was madness in their eyes as they searched for meat. Family pets, dogs, and cats rushed about, and then I saw a lion. It ran and leapt upon a man who was cornered near an alley. He screamed and screamed as the hungry lion devoured him. Then, I looked in horror as a child, not more than two years old, sitting in the street was attacked by a pit bull and torn apart. After the dog left, the rats and vultures finished off what was left.

Madness was everywhere. I walked by a house where a mother sat upon her porch, wild-eyed, eating something bloody and small. I called out to her, and asked what she ate. She looked at me with hollow eyes and cried out, insanely, "It's my child, I'm eating my child!" Suddenly, the earth started to rumble and I assumed it was another earthquake, but no, the earth opened up and out of a hole, the size of a large car, poured creatures. They were short, fat, many bald, and they had eyes that spun around insanely. Some were laughing hideously as they surveyed the scene before them; others were growling fiercely. They moved quickly out onto the street, and I was reminded of hell's bowels opening and of the mouth of hell widening, of hell enlarging itself. The creatures of horror scurried everywhere, grabbing unsuspecting people. There were shrill screams as men, women, and little children were dragged, some vomiting, some already dead, into the hole. It was so quick. I could hardly believe it had happened. The hole covered itself back up, and there was no sign that there had been a disturbance.

Then I saw more wild animals. Not only had circus cages opened and the wild beasts poured out, but also the genetic monsters that the scientists had engineered had escaped. There were many kinds, each seemed more horrible and bizarre than the last ... dog-like animals with many heads and eyes, with frothing mouths, looking all around for any kind of flesh to eat; weird snake-like creatures with rabbit-shaped heads slithered with lightening speed; porcupine-quilled animals with large horns on their heads, barely able to walk, lumbered along as a pregnant woman who is near her time of delivery. Then, there were the jellyfish-looking animals that hardly moved. Occasionally, as a person ran by in terror, they shot out venom, blistering him horribly until he died. The animal then moved slowly to the body and started to ingest it by sucking it up into his own body. There were also spiders everywhere. Small, new strains of spiders that killed instantly with their bite. The victim turned black, as if the blood in his veins had turned to coal. There were large, man-sized spiders that roamed freely, taking victims in their claws and stinging repeatedly. But the pain did not end even when the person escaped; the bite became a horrible boil-like, festering sore that was unbearably painful. There were so many other kinds of horrible animal life that it cannot be told here. Even the plants were deadly now, giving off toxic gasses that paralyzed and stung the victim to death.

There was so little food or water; people searched constantly for it. Even in the midst of horror, men driven by insane lust raped and murdered women and children, and even other men. Many criminals and insane people had escaped when the doors of institutions had flown open in the earthquakes. Even gangs of wicked women roved about, raping men and grabbing them as the women screamed, "I shall have your name! You are my husband." There was constant screaming and gunfire; death was the rule, life the exception. Some of the people cowered in houses hoping to hide themselves, but evil men carrying guns would run into the houses, dragging the people away, and then I'd hear screams or gunshots. There was a new breed of terrorist now; he carried small guns armed with toxic bullets. He only had to fire them near his victims, and instantly the people were paralyzed. Some less fortunates writhed, screaming, changing before my eyes into blob-like masses of melting flesh. There were people who were so diseased, they looked inhuman. The radiation from so much bombing had produced a race of insane, unearthly-looking creatures. They were horrible abominations like the creatures in a horror movie, but actually much worse; ghouls who would go through towns murdering and tearing people apart. Then, there were winds of searing heat that blew through cities and these were followed by freezing cold, for even the elements were confused.

Unbelievably, there were still those in the occult who were practicing their crafts, grabbing children and the helpless and doing new abominations to them, never before imagined by the mind of man, because the demons were literally standing by ready to instruct them.

Holes would open in the earth, like the hole in the sand that appears when a clam is beneath it. But these holes would open suddenly, and as a passerby walked along, he'd fall down a dark passageway into the arms of waiting demons, to be dragged screaming into Hell.

The landscape was stark like a naked woman. Where there had once been children's laughter, families, and people's businesses, now there was only stark desolation and atrocity. Even the Christians were dying, just as the sinners; those who had not really given themselves to God were counted with the sinners. There was disbelief everywhere.

Peoples' faces were darkened, and horror was in their eyes. Now and then, I could hear deep rumblings in the earth, and then the violent shaking would start, and the cracks would open up, from which more spiders, rats, snakes, owls, and evil creatures would emerge. For America the beautiful had become a habitation for owls and every evil creature. I looked as lava poured up out of the cracks, as if the whole earth rested upon a molten, volcanic Hell. Then, deeper rumblings, and utter darkness. The darkness blanketed everything in its path; a flood of putrid clotted blood-like darkness that killed with a terrible stench. After the darkness was past, new, deadly toxic winds blew through the towns and cities, killing everyone in their path. Those people who were left after so much devastation were ill with the plagues that the wind and darkness brought. People limped about screaming, many blinded, mutated, blackened by plagues. Mothers carrying dead children in their arms, their minds burned by the deadly chemicals, clawed at the air as if crying out for help, but there was none. Then the hailstones, rocks really, started to drop from the heavens, and the angel shielded me or I would have perished. There was no place to hide, because the stones broke through the roofs of houses, killing many who were hiding inside. The angels guided me to a mountainous area, and I saw once-strong men on their knees crying out to the mountains, "Fall on me," but the mountains did not obey.

The whole scene from beginning to end was horror and destruction beyond the imagination of man. The words I have spoken actually do no justice to the utter abomination that lies directly in the path of the world. There is so much more that awaits the nation of America and the world that I cannot name it here. Be assured of one thing: if you do not repent and turn to God, He will count you with the sinners and you will be destroyed. For He has been merciful to the undeserving for a very long time. He truly does see America's people's sins very clearly, and there is an hour of recompense ahead. Cry out to Him to save yourself and those you love and as many as will receive Him. For the hour is near, almost at the door now, when the land of your forefathers shall be plunged into darkness as has never been seen or conceived of by the mind of men.

HEAR ME, PEOPLES OF THE EARTH ...

great and terrible things are in store for you and your world. The spirit is churning and boiling because of what is about to be released upon mankind and the world. Things so utterly horrible are waiting for the exact moment for My angels and the devils to loose them upon a waiting planet and upon the soft and delicate flesh of man. For man is not tough, even though he thinks he is. He is puny and can be so easily torn apart. Man's only strength is in Me. Without Me, he is a cowering, cornered animal, ready for the kill. Man is vulnerable and not only in the flesh, but in the mind and spirit also.

I must tell you, sadly, that men's hearts will literally explode with the fear of what is about to be released upon a sleeping world and upon slumbering, dulled hearts. People have been lulled to sleep by their idols. TV, radios, videos, movies, and all the world's pleasures and riches have been a sleeping pill to the masses. Drugs have been the opium of many people, too. The cities are full of half-crazed, half-dead zombies who lifelessly walk the streets and haunt the underground, the underworld. In Europe and other parts of the earth, people go down into catacombs, underground tunnels, to perform all sorts of strange rituals. Witches all across your land, right under your noses, are doing such bizarre and horrible deeds, that I would not utter them. In houses next to you, little children are being horribly molested by beastly men. In yours and other nations, corrupt government politics are being practiced. There are many, many cover-ups and secret dealings going on, so many, in fact, that confusion reigns because no government or society can exist built on lies. No one knows who to trust or what to believe. Many top-secret experiments are going on, and if you knew the half of it, you would be horrified! New deadly, toxic germ warfare is being experimented with at an alarming speed. New plagues—never known to man—-much, much worse than AIDS, are being toyed with. For the spirit of Hitler did not die when he did. Unparalleled shortages and famines are shortly to fall upon man. When people are riddled by toxins from wrong eating habits and food that is poor in nutrients and are subjected to starvation, insanity is the next horrid step. When the body and brain are depleted by a lack of food, suddenly the toxins in the system flood it, overloading and literally poisoning it. There is not as much insanity from starvation in third-world countries, because they eat a much more natural diet than in America. So you can see that even the starvation process will be a terrible thing. With so much death, corpses will pile up, and the stench and disease will pollute the air, making it unsafe even to breathe.

But, I tell you now that all these natural horrors will be nothing compared to the demonic atrocities that shall plague the earth and man. Things never seen or thought of by the human mind are being conjured up by Satan right now. When he is released in fury upon your nation and world, chaos and unprecedented horror shall stalk you and your children. The underworld is aflame, seething and bubbling with the molten mind of the Devil over what lies ahead, for even the kind and gentle humans you are surrounded by. They won't last long in the face of fury and the terrorizing that shall chop and thresh your land. For the demons have a new and furious song in their hearts, and it is the song of "Annihilation!"

The earth that is now floating in space is presently intact, but soon, from waves of sin, she will shutter and creak, like a ship being plummeted in a furious gale, ready to go down into the dark depths of the sea. For your planet will shake, roll, and come apart from the battering of what is ahead. Earthquakes and, worst of all, earth-shakes of unparalleled magnitude will move even great mountains out of their places. Fetid, still, lifeless, yellow-gray air shall hover, as My angels hold back the cleansing winds that have kept your earth and air clean. The blessing of rain shall be stopped from gently falling. The insects will multiply horribly and will mutate into killing machines, and men will know, as they are being stung and bitten to death, that there is a righteous and angry God who can bear their perverted, evil wickedness no longer.

Where there was once prosperity and beauty in America—clean, neat homes and nicely dressed people going to work in beautiful, shiny cars, having coffee in awe-inspiring great skyscrapers, going home to play with the kids, having a peaceful Sunday brunch—these pleasant things shall be traded for holocaust. What the Jews suffered at Hitler's hands was a meek and mild picnic in the park compared to what is ahead.

Wake up America, wake up world, for even if you will not believe these words, it does not change truth. Even if you would hide your head in the sand, you cannot stop the tidal wave that shortly will pour across your path and your children's. My Holy Word says these things shall happen; Adam and Eve unlocked the box containing great horror, but My Son died so that you might live and survive what lies in the near future. I never wanted you to sip of death and fire. I would that no person should ever perish and drink the fire and damnation of Hell. I love man. I adore you, little creatures I have created. I am a Father who has made children with His hands. Just as you would die for your children, so I sacrificed Myself for you, for when I gave My Boy. I gave My heart, too, because My Boy had My heart. You also have My heart. I hover over you in love, whether you are a Christian or a sinner. I want you. It's so easy. Just tell Me you want My Son and Me, too. Cry out to Us before it's too late for you and your babies. Please, please, hear My Words; I am desperate that you would not turn away. The devil has had far, far too many of My created human beings that he has dragged screaming into Hell. That is not where you or your loved ones belong. It was not created for you or mankind, but for Satan. Whether you are a Christian or a sinner, listen to these words, for many people will die in what is ahead. Wake up, shake yourself. Pray and meditate upon My Word. Join Me in realms of Spirit where you are safe. Come up into My Holy Hill, up into My Spirit. You will know the way, for I shall show you, if you will attend unto My Spirit.

Pray this ... Father, you are so great and I am so small, yet you would scoop me up in Your hand and rescue me out of this dark world. Save me through what is ahead; lift me up into your Holy Hill where there is safety in Your presence. For You are wondrous and Your Spirit abides and overshadows man. You are the mother hen who hides Your little chicks beneath her wings. You are the breasted one who feeds her sucklings and enwraps Your little ones in her strong and gentle arms. You are the mighty and terrible one who pays back those who harm Your children, those who stubbornly resist You. You are the embodiment of love, even when You judge sin. You will show me great mercy as You have shown me all my days. You are mercy, even to the undeserving. You are sweet with the rapturous scent of love. You are a perfume because You are goodness and purity. You have longed for me and hovered over me even before I was born, even when I was only a thought in Your vast mind. And when I was birthed into this world, You saw and attended me and waited patiently for me. You are all in all, the beginning and end of all. You are Alpha and You are Omega, the first, the last. You are I Am. You are and shall be forever and because You live, I live. Take me up to You.

Rescue me. Grab me with Your strong arms away from evil, out of even the very sight of the enemy of my soul. Cover me with Your feathers that I am hidden in you, and You in me. Let the one who has tried to capture me and rip me away from You be at last put away from me forever. Enwrap me, swaddle me, engulf me in You, Heavenly One ... Daddy, I love you.

YOUR COUNTRY HAS BEEN INVADED BY A FOE ...

more deadly than the nuclear bomb or foreign soldiers invading your shores. The dangerous invader is PRIDE. America is bursting at its seams from pride. This arrogance is the "can do" mentality. This mentality says, "We're a rich nation; we control the world; we are, in fact, the skyscraper of the earth."

I have watched the peoples of your land from afar, as have My host of heaven, and I must confess, I am embarrassed at what I see. I have even felt that I would vomit your peoples out of the earth. If it were not for the intercessors in your land and also the heavenly intercessors, I would have destroyed you long ago.

Yours is the pride of Ancient Rome ... of the gallant, invincible gladiator. Yours is the arrogance of the senate forum, playing games of control with the world. For Rome thought she was the world and no one would stop her. But, alas, as all controllers and manipulators, she burned. Collapse was inevitable, for pride truly does go before a fall, and it will be a very great fall when America collapses.

I have watched in disgust as your government has played God and whore to other nations. I have blushed as I have watched the evil, little dictators destroying the poor and needy in your land. As I have watched the horror of abortion legislated in your land, I have wept for the darlings slit apart by the steel in the hands of wicked politicians. For their mouths drip saliva as they plan the murder of innocents ... those betrayers who kill for 20 silver pieces. These same men are planning to wipe out not only the babies of your country, but now the old, insane, feeble, retarded, and eventually, I tell you with sorrow, My own children. For Christian, you are next on their evil list. You are the highest priority on Satan's hit list, because you are Mine. The "New Laws" governing the killing of undesirables will eventually be passed, and real persecutions will begin in America.

People will weep and mourn when they see the great city of America fall, and very great will be her fall. Where else in the world is there a country with so many great cities? I tell you, these cities of skyscrapers and hustling, arrogant, "can do people" will not survive the fire ahead. Searing, melting torment shall cleanse your land, and the pompous, little people who run about shall burn, too. They will be amazed when they see the destruction ahead, because they believed they were gods, invincible, human-ists. Their little theories of man are all sealed up, perfect and set in granite. Their evil ideas are their religion.

They think, "If your lover and you have sex, don't get pregnant. If you do make a mistake, run to the clinic down the street and take care of 'it'." Oh, the shame!" That "it" was a beautiful seed placed by My tender hand into the secret reaches of her Mother. They say, as they leave their sterile offices, "Let's do lunch," and they shall do lunch when they "sip fire" for their eternal meal forever and ever. They say, "Mom and Dad are old; shove them into a nursing home. We never need see them again. They're used up, and we have used them as much as we needed them." Remember, I say to honor your parents. I am not playing a sweet game when I tell you these things. They say, "Let's go get some porno films, take some drugs, and watch movies," from the pits of Hell, sent up to men to educate their minds to evil. All these evils and more are corrupting the fields of men's hearts throughout the land. All this is and shall be, more and more, with each day that passes, a horror story.

But I must tell you, I am even angrier with some in My church. You ministers who pervert My Word for gain, who will not say what I tell you to say, are become My enemies. You who lead many astray by doctrines of men and devils are soon to also sip of death, lest you repent and turn back to Me in uncompromising honesty. Do not fear man, fear Me, because I can suddenly send you to Hell. People's lives hang in the balance and you can save them with your words. Many look to you for truth. They should look to Me, but they are true sheep, "following the leader." If the leader falls, they do, too. You must teach them to survive, even physically, what is coming.

The end of American life as you now know it is at hand. The days grow evil and dangerous from, "Sea to Shining Sea." Oh, America, how I would gather you up into My arms and clutch you to My breast and stop what is about to fall upon you, but you would not. But I say, with mercy and love still in My heart for you, "Lift your eyes to the hills from whence cometh your strength." Cry aloud, shout to Me in the far reaches of heaven. Cry out for the help of "The Breasted One," the all-sufficient one, that in the "Day of Calamity," that will surely fall upon America the Beautiful, you and your children would be saved and know "Your God Reigns." Know also, that if you repent and turn from your wickedness, I will rescue you with the power in My hand.

SECTION 7

MY ANGELS LITERALLY COVER YOUR EARTH

There are as many of them as there are sands on the shores. In some cases, they stand shoulder to shoulder. Usually, where there are this many of them in an area of the earth, it is because great protection is desperately needed. Always they are on the earth for My purposes. Their main objective is to protect people; however, they have many other jobs, too. Sometimes they protect animals as well. If it were not for My angels, the earth would have perished long ago. You see, they are an extension of My hand in the world. Doesn't My Word say the power is in My Hand? That power is made up of light. So, too, then, My angels are filled with My power and light.

But what I want to speak to you about is the angels whose job it is to wait for "your words" and then zoom up to Me so that I can bring them to pass. Because these angels are filled with My glory, or love power in action, they hope that the words you and others speak will be good ones. The angels take no joy when you use your tongue in an evil manner and then I have to follow suit and bring evil into your life. The reason I created this principle was so that I could bless you, not curse you. Listen to your words. How many times have you said, "I don't have any money. I'm broke." Have you considered what you are really speaking? You are saying, God is unable to supply my needs. Have you considered what the word "broke" implies? It really says you are "broken." This says you are a broken man. There is a good way of being broken, that is, when you are putty in My hands. But there's also another type of being broken, and that is not good. This brokeness says, "I am powerless and so is My God. Of course, other factors come into play, including obedience and work, as far as prosperity is concerned. But you must, above all, desire good things to come into you and your families' lives.

In your hand and mouth is blessing or cursing, life or death. Did you really hear Me? You have a choice, life or death. Because the man is the head of the family, he has a special anointing. His words are power-filled. He is the priest of his home. What does a priest do? He ministers to the people under him. He is a leader; he has authority and power in his special job. It is a very important job, too. Being a husband is difficult in many instances because life has gotten tricky. Just to be able to make it through life in your world, especially in the days you are in, takes knowledge and wisdom and a real anointing from Me, the Father. There are so many obstacles in life these days. A person can be concentrating on one area and before he knows it another weed has sprung up in an unexpected area. So he goes over to pull that weed, but then another weed pops its head up in another area.

That is why it is so important to be talking to Me all the time. You desperately need My guidance and will need it even more in the turbulent days ahead. My people need knowledge. Do you remember the scripture, "My people die for lack of knowledge?" I did not say for lack of wisdom. Wisdom is knowing what to do with the knowledge you acquire. If you don't know there are cures for cancer, then you could suffer for it. If you don't know how to do your taxes, you could get into trouble. Your earth is overrun with knowledge, yet it can be tricky to acquire it. There is so much knowledge that it can be difficult to know where to go to find it. Your world is like a large maze and you and all humanity are the mice in the maze. You want to reach the middle, the prize of the high calling but the middle is not in view. So then, you have to try to blindly move from place to place trying to win in life's game.

Think of how you felt when you began that business venture, full of hope and joy. It probably wasn't what your heart really longed to do, but you had such high hopes for you and your family. Then you discovered there were going to be problems and challenges, hard ones. So, because your heart really was never in it, you quit and tried something else, however, the same thing happened. Many people spend and I do mean spend, their lives in this pattern. Just like throwing money into a wishing well. Their multiple marriages follow this principle as do their jobs and finances. They really are gambling and losing at the game board of life. Because they are not grounded and anchored to Me, they float from one phase to another.

There is a pattern and it is called the spirit of "deja vous." Have you ever known that the phase, "been there, done that," is working in your life? It seems that you have repeated situations in your life over and over again. This is not good. This is the spirit of being the tail and not the head. For the tail is a foul, odorous, worm infested place while the head gets the goodies: delicious food, beautiful smells, gorgeous sights, glorious sounds, and precious thoughts. You don't want to have to keep repeating your life's lessons. This is not a fun, exciting place to be. If this is where your are, you need healing in your mind, spirit and body.

"What does it take to get healed?" you ask. I reply, "Whatever it takes." Whether you go to a counselor on a regular basis or a person skilled in deliverance and inner healing or you fast and pray, there is no stopping till the work is done. You must not become afraid and give up. Yes, there will be great sorrow, for many of you have suffered abuse as children, but you must still continue till healing is complete. You don't want to continue as you have, for if you do, you will perish. Maybe you won't die in your body, but your spirit will crumble. You will lose hope. You never want to despair of life. You must learn your lessons. You must allow yourselves to know the truth even though it is gruesome. The angels are standing by waiting for your faith-filled words. All of heavens' angels stand ready to help and assist you. You have armies at your disposal.

I do not wish to see you suffer anymore. You have suffered enough. Many of you have suffered from what others
have done to you. It was totally unfair, but because of your
genealogy, you were prey for Satan. Because of the laws I
have set up, I could not stop the abuse against you, but I did
have a rescue plan. My Son's blood and your words mixed
together will become a healing balm of Gilead, to you.

Legions of angels are at My command and at yours. Your
words are a creative force that I specifically made so that
you could use your voice to bless yourselves and your families and others. You have the Holy One living in you. You have
the body of Christ; you have music and praise and a host of
other things that I have meant to arm you with against the
world. For, I want you to be rich and prosperous, have a truly
happy family, be supernaturally healthy and filled with joy. I
want it all for you. The whole ball of wax, the good life, the
total deal. Just as your father wanted good things for his little one so too, I want you to walk in a supernatural glory.
When you pass by, I want people to say, "He used to have
some real problems in his life, but would you look at him
now. He is truly one of the blessed ones of God. Look how
handsome he is, look at his beautiful clothes, and his gorgeous family. Look at that beautiful car and lovely home he
lives in. Look at the glory and peace on his face. His God did
all that, for him. He wasn't always like that. It's as if God
brought him back from the dead. Look at how powerful that
man is when he speaks, people truly do listen. He and his are
truly blessed, truly blessed by God."

You have an arsenal at your right hand for you are My
representative, My son in the earth. I want to parade you so
that people know who I Am. I want to win others through
your success. Talk to Me when you make plans. Stay in touch.
When I tell you to move, move. For I long to show you off as
My completed product, My glory child. A child of the King of
Kings and Lord of Lords, the one who owns the cattle on a
thousand hills.

WHEN ADAM WAS IN HIS GARDEN, HE WAS PROTECTED FROM ALL

manner of evil. But Adam fell from the glory of knowing Me. He became a wanderer in a dreary land. Man has wandered in Adam's harsh footsteps a long time. Man has plodded down a muddy road of hardships. The cross has been the only real way out of man's rutted road. Still, man has only been able to go so far and to reach so high. The mountain peaks have been there, but few have made it to the top. Most have only gone halfway, or even less. The hinds' feet have slipped and fallen and have not been able to go up slippery heights, and have fainted, even before the climb began, or have come to rough obstacles, and have slipped back. It seems when they've gained a foot, they've fallen back a foot and a half. The mountain's been so very big and they've been so small, and the climb has been so rough. The mountain is a mountain of hope and My promises. My children have had a few promises fulfilled, but not many.

Why? First, they've been afraid to be alone in their homes with Me. The world has always pressed in. The lure of things, people, and places has been a real temptation. Then, My people have placed themselves under the law instead of under grace. They have not realized that they are kings and princes in My Kingdom and in My Army. Then, the hour has been late and Satan has been at work so hard.

But I would not be God if I did not cause a people to be holy and righteous enough to walk up the mountain into the joy of the peaks, to walk right up to the high places with Me. There have never been a people there before. There have been a few stragglers, but not a whole people. These people shall be the Army of God. They shall rule from their high places. They shall win, never fail. On their way up, they shall leave encumbrances behind; anything that is heavy and useless shall be left for the final ascent. It shall lighten their climb. They will feel a release from the weight of it.

The people of earth shall be amazed as they watch My children. For the earth is not worthy of them, My Holy Ones. When they break through the clouds of the summit, clouds that have blinded their eyes to where the top lay, they shall break forth into joy, and when they put their precious feet upon the top, their joy shall be full. Yes, "they shall go out with joy and be led forth with peace, the mountains and the hills shall break forth before them; there'll be shouts of joy and all the trees of the fields shall clap their hands."

In the morning, when you arise, the light has dispelled the darkness of night. That is how it will be when you win. A great day of rejoicing forevermore shall be upon you, a joy that shall reach heaven. For the joy has been prepared in heaven by Me. It's taken a long time. The climb's been rough, almost impossible, like a child struggling and struggling to be born in a long, hard labor. Doesn't the mother rejoice when the child is born and forget the terrible birth? Her joy is full. So it shall be with you, daughter of Zion.

I have prepared great things to warm your heart, great things that you know not. Joys that you can't imagine now. Be grateful, not all will have the victory you shall have. Not many will see what you shall see or hear what you shall hear. For a victory day and march await you, and they're only the start of what's prepared. Take hope, take joy.

Meditate on these things. I haven't forgotten you. You are the apple of My eye, sweet princess.

Have hope and wait just a little while. I can do above what you'd dare to hope. Meditate on My goodness and these words. Believe them. They're life!

MY LITTLE ONE, YOU'VE PAID A GREAT PRICE ...

for your loved ones and Me. I wish to give to you a new joy, a new walk, a new day, a new family. It can happen quickly because I am God, Jehovah, "the God who heals you." I can make all things new. Doesn't My Word say this?

Up, up into your high places, away from all the dirtiness of earth, up to new heights, you shall fly. As the ram and mountain goats travel in high places, so can you all be effortlessly, freely, joyously dancing on the mountains of your heights. We're there and will be with you and yours in new dimensions.

MY PEOPLE HAVE WANDERED IN A DESERT EXISTENCE

Sins and ignorance of Myself have separated them from Me. The desert is an unkind land. It's hot and dusty and traveled by few people. The heat beats constantly and creates spiritual thirst that won't be quenched. Many paths lead into desert living, rebelliousness and hatred and love of self are just some of the paths. Sins of the forefathers have made steady paths through generations of families.

My people have died for lack of knowledge, but it is not that they haven't heard My Anointed Word. Many have been unable to grasp the true depths of My Spirit. My Holy Spirit has striven to teach by My anointing. Their minds have heard, but they have been unable to digest what they have heard and use it in new energy forces. In desert living, there are continuous dangers. Bandits are always stalking, stealing what little My people have had, hence the scripture, "What little they have, shall be taken from them." And yet, there is still beauty in the desert. For where I am, there is beauty. White sands and blood-red sunsets soften the harshness, for I would not leave My people helpless and alone; I am always with them. I long to see My tried, tired and thirsty people soaked in water and brought from wilting into refreshing wholeness.

As the caravan trudges along, suddenly they see in the distance a lovely oasis: My Spirit repose oasis. In the distance, they can see tall, lush palms laden with nourishment, and as they near, they see thirst-quenching waters. As they stumble and run to the garden and enter a place of great beauty, joy awaits then. Pools so deep and clear flow with My Spirit. Sit down, My children, there to be ministered "to." For I have set servant angels there to treat you as the royalty that you are. Your every need and whim are their delight to give you, that your limp spirits would stand tall, filled with all manner of joy. There your wounds will heal in a moment. There is sweet peace in the "Glades of My Spirit Garden," and sweet-smelling odors perfume the gentle breezes. For My Spirit always blows gently through the garden. On the winds is carried the scents of the "Fruits of the Spirit" ... and I will sit with My children and eat with them of those "fragrant fruits." Fruits are not just to look at, but also to eat. For in communion ceremonies, We shall eat of the "Tree of Life" and of the representation of the invigorating body and blood of My Dear Son. In the garden, you will find Spirit truths you never dreamed of and manifestations of the Spirit Realm that you cannot imagine. There is great joy there beyond imaginings. And that is only the first realm. The higher the realms, the more beautiful and perfect the joy.

I'll lead you there, and My flock will follow; My True Flock. Yes, you've been scattered, little flock, but I shall bring you in. Just the joy of being together and of one mind and able to communicate joyously together will be so lovely for you, My children.

I can hardly wait for the joy we'll have. I have a present for you that I long to have you open. We've waited so long and it's right around the corner. Take joy and hope as new garments, for it shall be soon.

RESTORATION

There is a rhythm to life, a natural ebb and flow. Like the ocean's tides that cause the waves to be sucked out to sea and then turn on themselves and rush to the shore. Here is a mystery. Which do you think the waters prefer to flow to, the shore or the deep? You and other people are on the shore. Most people live on land. But the ocean depths are the source, or home, of the great waters. Amazingly, they prefer and ever flow toward land. True, there is a great pulling of the mighty waters into the ocean depths, but more than that, there is a greater pull to the shores. Actually, it is a miracle that the deep does not hold the waters from reaching out to the land in the form of tides. With the depth and weight of the water and whirlpools and undertows, it is indeed My Spirit that moves the majestic oceans to shore. Why do I do this? I do it for you. For everything on your planet Earth has been custom-made for you.

Consider a custom-built home. Everything in that house is designed particularly for the new owners, especially in the most expensive ones. Every detail is created for the future occupants' wishes. Nothing is left to chance. Great planning goes into every aspect of the design. Much of the time, the most fun part of the whole process is in the fine-tuning of the home. Those last small details, the amenities, accessories, are what really add individuality and turn a house into a home.

So it was with Earth. Here's a little cosmic joke. I accessorized! It's true. I added all the lavish, splashy wonders of the earth not just for practical purposes, but also for your pleasure. I wanted to bless you, to thrill and excite your senses, to pleasure you!

You know, I really want My people to hear Me say this. Listen now! I did not create My children to be drab, religious, boring nerds! And yet, that seems to be the mindset of the church as a whole. Holiness is not being nerds. Holiness is about the condition of the heart. Holiness is about true goodness. It's about where your priorities are, where your affections and loyalties lie! It comes down to whose side you are on, the enemy's or Mine. So choose you this day life or death, blessing or cursing!

Again, I did not create a passionless people. On the contrary, I am a passionate God. I created you, My children, to have bodies like those in the animal kingdom, flesh, blood, bones, but an eternal spirit like Mine. Isn't that thrilling! I gave you not just one dimension, but two: supernatural, and physical, or natural. You have a mind, too, but it is part of the natural. The point I want to make is this. Be passionate! Do all things with great relish. Do them well. This goes for sex, too. For you who are married, make sex beautiful. Fill it with love and joy. Let there be no forcefulness or roughness in it. You men should be the greatest wooers of your brides there have ever been. You should be the great lovers, like the King in the "Song of Solomon." You should make your wife want you because of your kindness to her inside and outside the bedroom. Did you hear Me? You are to treat My princesses as just that—royalty. For that is exactly who they are. This is not just a pretty description of them. I am very pointed and serious about this. They truly are My Royal Queens of the earth. In the Spirit, they are adorned in regal garb. I see them dressed in purple with long trains of gold. Their hair is braided with jewels, and atop their heads sit glistening golden crowns. Soon, they will put on white robes that are bright as the sun and walk with Me in faraway places. And I will be their Husband and King.

For these women were My little babies, My little girls. I wish no harm to ever come to them. I say again, I wish no harm to come to them. Woe unto those who harm one of these little ones.

There are rhythms to life. There is rhythm in a baby's breathing as he sleeps so innocently upon his bed. There is a rhythm to your walking, running, talking, laughing. Rhythm is everywhere in all aspects of life, even in machines. Computers and cars alike are metered in rhythm. For rhythm is a part of time, and time is a part of eternity and a part of Me. The seasons emanate from the rhythm of time.

Everything has a season, time, and rhythm. For I am a great creator of order. I love orderliness, cleanliness, neatness. In Eden, there were no weeds, thistles, or thorns. Eden was scrupulously clean. It was orderly—simplicity in diversity. Things ran well there —perfectly. The plants and animals were simple, clean-cut, yet there were a huge number of them. Life was simple for Adam and his wife. They had no worries or fears. Why should they? There was nothing to fear or worry about. That is why they could be so peaceful. All their needs in every minute detail, as well as their desires, were attended to by Me. They were in heaven—heaven on earth.

When they fell, they lost their natural rhythm, their sync, with Me. They went over to the enemy's side for only one beat, one heartbeat, and that's all it took to destroy humanity. I saw their eyes when they left the godly rhythm of their lives. They flickered! In that horrible, horrendous, hideous moment in eternity, time actually stood still. The pupils of their eyes reflected not My image, but that of the Beast. And I hated Lucifer with a righteous, unending hatred. At that moment in time, I vowed I would take eternal vengeance upon the one who stole My beloved children from Me. And, alas, I will crush the head of the serpent totally when his time is fully come. And each of you must crush him in your own lives. When people give pasty, anemic sermons about putting on the full armor of God, it makes Me want to spew. This scripture passage is not a sweet little retort about putting on a little faith here and a little bit of the Word there. This is a scream in the Spirit, a crying out, a direct order to a solider. Just as if in the natural, war had been declared, and an officer went in to his men and loudly told them to suit up, an army was on its way to get them, to overpower, overthrow, crush them. Well, so it is with you. The time is ripe; the time is now! You are that solider, that army. You are just about to be attacked in the night. Quickly get into your suit of armor so you can be protected and fight the good fight, so you can win.

I am with you even until the end of the age.

Don't be afraid, little flock, for it is the Father's good pleasure to give you the keys to the kingdom. These are the keys that let you get through the gates and into paradise, in the Spirit Realm, even before you finally come home to be with your God forever and ever. These are the keys to your life. These keys open up Realms of the Spirit so that you can walk in and take back the territory the enemy has stolen from you. Do you hear Me? Once again I say, I give you the keys to aid you in your life to overcome the enemy. These keys are truths, Kingdom Truths, that have been at times hidden from you, just like losing your car keys. You have to look for them, but at last you find your keys. So it is with Kingdom Keys. They were always there, always yours, but you just had to search for them, like pearls of great price. If I made it too easy for you humans, you would not value them. So I made it like children who hunt for berries in the woods. They take their little baskets and gather the precious fruit, piece by piece. Then when their baskets are full of fragrant, glistening fruit, the children run excitedly home to give them to their families. So it is with you, chosen ones. I wish to give you the Keys to the Kingdom, so that you can run with them and share them with the rest of the family so that they can be readied first for war and then for the great joy of the next step, eternal joy with their Father, God.

STRONG MEAT IS FOR THE STRONG

For stouthearted men shall rule My Kingdom. As an earthly ruler, I would not give control of the kingdom to the faint, for strength becomes a mighty ruler. Quiet, gentle strength is a great weapon in times of trouble. A knowledge that nothing can overcome is what I want to instill into My people.

The strong man's feet are prepared for war. His weapons

are cleaned and polished. He is adorned with his armor and boosted in the spirit by his comrades and sent with blessings into the heat of battle.

My people shall conquer. My people are "conquistadors." When the heat of battle rages, they shall stand and not fall. Though they see 10,000 fall, they shall stand.

My army that the prophets foretold shall be of a strength that will make the greatest world armies look weak. Behind their every move, their every maneuver, shall be the Creator God. Jehovah is My name. I am strong in battle. I am a strong anointer. The oil flows from My hand, strong and true. A fire is in the oil. A fire shall fall from heaven upon My army, not a consuming fire, but an anointing blazing fire.

It shall purge and give superhuman strength. It shall prepare the soldier for battle. The pitchers are full of oil; the anointing cup, the presses and vats hold oil to the overflowing. Streams of oil shall flow from the throne room, rivers of oil shall engulf men. From above the earth it shall come. Living oil, rejuvenating, restoring, healing, preparing, repossessing oil. Oil that shall flow back through time as a river and carry to the present, lost things: moneys, lands, happinesses stolen by the enemy, things that have been forgotten, things you haven't even known, you've lost, but I knew. I watched and have waited to replenish and replace.

A creative fire is in the oil. Your children, so dear to you and so sweet, so precious to Me too, shall receive blessings from above. I have watched their darling faces as they've slept upon their beds. I have watched them patiently and known a day of retrieving things lost to them would arrive.

For things, even spiritual things have been stolen from all My people, but a bringing-back hour is here. I shall go into spaces in eternity and bring back the spoils to My little ones, and hearts shall leap. Hearts shall leap! For a joy shall fill your land. For in the oil are fulfilled promises. Promises, I shall fulfill. Promises as yet unfulfilled. In the

oil is soothing and relaxation. Like a massage. Relaxing and
stimulating. Relaxation, rejuvenation, stimulation, exulta-
tion, regeneration, all these shall I provide My children. The
times shall speed ahead. Time shall speed as if on an oiled
road, speeding ever faster, producing more and more heat
and velocity. Until time shall not exist, only the quiet dimension of God and man. There is a knowing, there is a knowing
presence that goes beyond words. Where words are not only
not needed, but would not achieve anything. There is a quiet
silent knowing place, a place so sacred, a place where man
can slip in and not need to even think. There is a place as if
in a vacuum of time, away from everything except My Spirit,
a completely safe, completely reverent quiet place. It is
beyond the stars, beyond time, beyond angels and men,
beyond everything, a place where only One resides. A Spirit
Place. You must go there for a time because you are battle
weary, My People, My Daughter. The fighting's been heavy,
the battle constant. I will help you into that place and Our
Spirits will mingle. Into the place beyond all places. You and
I alone, together.

At last, Our Marriage will be consummated in Spirit and
in Truth. As in the quiet of an earthly bedroom, there We
shall dance the dance of lovers. Our Spirits shall unite in
wedded bliss. In Holiness shall We, at last, become completely one.

Now daughter, sleep this night with a promise upon your
pillow. The glories to come shall erase the ugliness of the
past. When the oil washes over you, warm and comforting, it
shall be a very, very great joy. No eyes have seen, no ears
heard, what I have prepared for you.

SOUND THE ANCIENT INSTRUMENTS

Tune the instruments of praise that the King of Glory
may come in. Who is the King of Glory? It is I, the Ancient
One, the Holy of Holies!

Lift Me up, oh ye gates! Lift Me up, oh ye doors, that the King might arise with healing in His wings! Lift Me up, oh cherubim, lift Me up angelic ones! Lift Me up, oh four and twenty elders! Lift Me up, all the holy host of all the ages! And lift Me up, high above the earth, oh daughter of Zion; for one day all men will speak My name with reverence, even those who will not serve the King.

I walk through heavenly corridors and chambers, readying them for My bride. For My Bride-People will one day walk into the courts of heaven and into the Bridegroom's arms, never to be separated again. So lift Me up, for you have reason to glory, oh ye worshippers. For when the Son takes a Holy wife, she shall be adorned in fine raiment, she shall be adorned in robes and gowns of adoration. She shall forever praise the goodness of the King.

She will walk in wonder at the glories, she will see through universes and galaxies. She will see future extravaganzas and ancient cities. She will look through passages of time and distance where angels pass. She will explore the Sea of Crystal and waterfalls of diamonds—crystalline waters. She will look into new and lovely realms of heaven's portals where cherubs and dolphins play. She will see snow-tinged mountains of high majesty and slide down snowfields and glaciers, riding the wind. She will dive into pools of new colors and swim under prisms of colors and play with the creatures below. She will walk down roads of stars and fly through new planets lit by the Holy Light of the Son, where there are bright shootings of flashing, lovely colors never imagined by the mind of man.

And when she returns from adventurous joy playing in the universe, what glory to come into the Kingdom of her Father and His Son and The Spirit. What joy when she comes into the Castle and Kingdom of her God! The attending maids and servant angels shall drape her in Royal Purple and fine linens and jewels in her hair and shall set her crowns upon her head. Then she shall walk regally to the throne of her Husband and they shall commune and laugh with joy at the beauty that shall always be forever and ever.

Though earth's roads seem hard, little flock, hold onto these words. Not too much longer, and We'll be together in glory.

THERE IS COMING A PEOPLE ...

who will be My answer to Satan's, "New World Order." They are My new order of humans, My called. They shall be My anointed ones, My "Army of Joel, the Army of the Lord, the Sons of God, the Saviors, Lights of the world, and Salt of the Earth." They will be the Firebrands who shall do wondrous things too great to tell. They will be a sweet smelling savor unto Me, their Abba Father. They will take the earth for Me and the people of earth who turn to Me through the reviving fire; in many instances, they will have this company of people to thank for their salvation. These lofty people are My little Jesuses.

The words that proceed out of their mouths shall be so power-filled that the earth, and devils, and people shall quake and tremble at the sound of their voices. They will command the elements of earth. Fire will spring forth, ablaze in crackling heat, when they say only a word. At their command, boulders resting on flat surfaces of the ground will begin to roll and will gather great speed like waves of the ocean breaking forth. Floods and tidal waves will spring up at the pointing of their fingers. And with the raising of their precious hands, hurricanes will begin to blow across the land.

Even the greatest demons will scurry away from them in utter horror and terror. And when the Word of God is spoken, great armies of Hell reserved for the last days will literally melt like candles before their eyes.

People everywhere will hear about these holy ones, and

they will either rejoice or wail.

These children of Mine, these called ones, chosen before the foundations of the earth were formed, will have the anointing of ... The Mind of Christ. Do you have any idea what that entails? The Mind of Christ is limitless, fathomless. It is all knowledge—past, present, future. It is full to bursting of the wisdom of the ages; it is creative and incredibly inventive. It is able to speak and out of nothingness—whatever is spoken appears, supernaturally. This is the "Creative Word." It is what I spoke when the world was formed. The heavens appeared in all their glory and life sprung forth. Because I will be able to trust these children of Mine, totally, I will give them total power in the earth. I created the earth for them anyway. All that I am speaking is just a glimpse of what is to come for the anointed of the Lord. The things I have spoken are only a taste of what is to be. These warriors will open doors into realms of Spirit and into realms of the earth that people do not even know exist. The supernatural power that they shall walk in will be pure light, pure glory, and wonder. People who are evil will drop in death, like flies, when the shadow of one of these anointed ones passes over them. Likewise, others will be instantly healed of every single illness and affliction in a moment from these "saviors." In and out of the natural and unseen Spirit Realms, these warriors shall pass effortlessly. They are My supernatural beings of light. Comets and asteroids will fall upon earth at their command. At the sound of their voice, rivers will reverse their flow and flow in the opposite direction. With an outstretched hand, oceans shall become bone dry. With a word, whole graveyards will spring to life, and those who were dead shall live, and many will repent. Many Lazaruses shall appear, worshipping and praising My Holy Name.

Many evil men, especially the Satanic ones, will be startled, then utterly horrified, when they turn to see "My Spirit Police" enter their vile camps. They will try to run, in utter

terror, but will be frozen into pillars of stony salt. Others
will be instantly hurled into hell by just the pointing of My
children's fingers. Other unrepentant ones will instantly
catch fire and become infernos. These cherished ones of
Mine will be given My power over snakes, serpents, and
devils.

These children are My "glory people," full to the brim-
ming of the oil of anointing, gladness, and healing.

Just as Jesus willingly laid down His life, they will willingly turn parts of the world over to evil. They will allow
the Antichrist to finally have control over the world, yet
they will travel about doing wondrous things even as
Moses did before Pharaoh. For believe Me when I say, "The
Antichrist is just a tool that I created as a necessity for the
end of the Age." He is only a pesky gnat that obeys Me ultimately and, like a surly dog, slinks over to Me when I call. I
could destroy him with only a thought or the blink of My
eye if I so desired. My army will not have a moment of fear
at the sound of his voice or at the sight of his Antichrist
system. These children of Mine who have walked through
the fire will fear nothing except Me. The fear they will have
for Me shall not be a horror, but a glory to them, for out of
respect and love for Me will come the knowledge of who I
really am. No man has ever really known Me like My Son
has; likewise, these "Sons" will know who "I Am that I Am,
is." And therefore, just the knowledge of who "I Am" will be
enough for them to set the world on fire with My Spirit, like
a mighty roaring blaze illuminating the darkness of a
blackened world. They shall go through the earth with the
"Sword of the Word" proceeding from their mouths and
destruction shall follow. Yet, best of all, the great love they
will possess shall do mighty things and all creation and the
trees of the field shall clap their hands and rejoice as they
pass by.

REMEMBER THE SONG ...

"This is the year of Jubilee?" The words to it are, "This is the year of jubilee, when all the captives are set free. Come you halt, you blind, you lame, come and shout for joy again. This is the year of jubilee."

The essence of this song is this, "During the year of jubilation, health, wealth, and joy will be restored one hundred fold, and even more, with faith."

You haven't sung this song for a long time and neither has My church. They are about to not only sing it, but they are about to "shout for joy again."

In Israel, when the "Year of Jubilation" fell upon the people, there was wild joy. All debts were canceled. But, even better, there was a sin absolution by the priests and rabbis. There was a "Corporate Cancellation of Sin." People began to get well, to heal, in their bodies, minds, and spirits, and unabashed, riotous, unrelenting "Joy" filled the nation of Israel. There was exultant celebrating. The people danced in the glory cloud of God. They broke bread and feasted on the wonderful new foods they could now afford to buy. They praised Me because suddenly the crippled could walk, run, and dance. The blind could at last see, and the deaf could now hear the beauty of the glory music.

Oh, such joy filled the land. It truly was a taste of heaven. Milk now flowed again in the land and the honeycomb spilled her sweet nectar upon My people. Once again, they could say, "He will be our God, and we will be His people."

Youth was restored, too, because that kind of a joyous outpouring breaks the spirit of agedness. The people became so strong in their bodies because "The joy of the Lord is my strength." Did you notice I said not your joy, but the "Joy of the Lord" gives strength? That is the joy I gave them, the joy of the Son, Jesus. It was not just a natural human joy, but it was a supernatural joy. Did you hear? It was beyond what your world could ever give you. Your world's joy has to do with things: prosperity, family, fun, etc. These are not bad; they are good, but they have a natural, earthly limit. However, this unearthly joy, this limitless wonder, is what is about to hit your planet and My people in an earth-shattering way, It will so far exceed any pittance of joy in comparison to what was poured out in times of old. You will have to blink; you will have to pinch yourself because of the glory of joy that is shortly to come upon My church.

There will be shouting in the streets. The earth will literally "open up and praise Me." When this happens, the "hidden things" will begin to flow out and shoot up from the depths of the earth. Incredibly rich oil stores will shoot forth; veins of diamonds and rare jewels will show themselves; rich mineral deposits, worth many kings' ransoms, will appear, and buried treasures, long forgotten and beyond your wildest dreams, will be discovered by you. Other, even more mysterious wonders, buried for eons, will come to you. Oh, the wonder and glory you will experience! It will be a supernatural outpouring of such unearthly magnitude that you could not contain it, if it were told to you. The mystery and wonder of it will be so glorious, so exciting, and just plain fun, that I smile down upon you from heaven.

Remember when you were a child what it was like to go on, or just to read about or even watch a treasure hunt on T.V.? Well, get ready for the fun and joy of your lives.

Then, when you add to this great and total healing and new youth and strength and outpourings of My Spirit so unbelievable, that human words cannot even begin to express, you have revival, restoration in all its wonder and glory.

Never has there been nor will there be anything to compare to this "Glory-Shoot, this Love-Fest, this oneness with God, upon planet Earth. Even the rocks and trees shall shout for joy. Yes, My creation will not even be able to contain itself. You will see the lion and adder praising Me together with you.

Jubilation is about to break out upon the land in a mighty torrent of Spirit Rain, and the Anointing Winds are just about ready to blow across your land! Hang on now, for you are about to experience the "explosion, the Anointing Fire of God!" JUBILATION, JUBILATION, JUBILATION upon My children!

BEAUTY

When a person has been through a lot of ugliness in his or her life, beauty is needed. Their soul craves beauty, splendor, loveliness. The worse the ugliness of their life is, the more beauty is needed to counteract it. My Word says, "I will give you beauty for ashes."

Unfortunately, the most loving, dedicated, loyal, and deep children of Mine have suffered the most. If I could only convey one thing to you, My little one, it would be this. I adore you! I love you so! Let all eternity, all universes, ring with the sound of My Words. I LOVE YOU! Let the winds whisper it. Let the breezes turn to gales, calling out your name! Let the stars twinkle and fall enraptured by My Love for only you, My precious, precious one. Let the North call to the South, the East to the West that you are My beloved. For I AM enraptured by you; I am utterly taken by you, My creation.

You see, you are the sun and moon to Me, the fiery red sunset, the heavens, rich and dark with wonder, the heady, smoking incense on the altar, cool green meadows, the nimble stag on the mountaintop. You are lofty and noble, great and wondrous, beautiful beyond human beauty. You are to Me, supernatural. You light My eye and you warm My heart.

Don't ever be afraid to love ME, because I am not a man. I do not ever reject you. You are in My Heart forever and ever. I made My creation in an array of hues like the colors of the earth: red, yellow, black, brown, white. I found pleasure in your creation. None of you are inferior. Each one of you is different, like falling snow. You are all beautiful to Me. I see beyond your exterior and into your hearts. I watch the very beating of your sweet little hearts in your chests. For I placed that heart into your waiting body and breathed My life into you when you were yet in your mother's womb. I watched you grow from a minute seed, a miracle, into a tiny baby. I was the real Father who waited for you to be born. I oversaw every second of the birthing. I experienced great joy when you were born. Whether you had an earthly daddy or not doesn't matter, because you had a Father and it was ME. I love you perfectly. I know you have no idea in your humanness what that means, but I know.

I love you with great sacrifice. I love you with great passion, as a sculptor loves the statue he has created and calls it very, very good. I love you tenderly as a mother, touching the cheek of her sleeping child. I love you unabashedly, as the artist of all creation, splashing colors upon your world and all eternity. I love you all in all.

None of you must ever fear death, for I will be there to hold your hand and bring you to My bosom. In fact, you should look forward to the day when we will at last be together. I would, however, rather catch you away, so that you would not have to taste death. I would prefer to translate you from your world to the next, or better yet, that you would walk upright into the millennial kingdom. However, when I see you again, it will be a family reunion.

Try to be happy in the meantime. Be good to yourself and others. Be loving and humble. Live each day with joy and gusto. Appreciate everything good. Open your eyes wide. See the world I have given you. Look at life afresh. Applaud others. Love the people you walk among, really love them, unselfishly, like I love you.

I want nothing from you except your love. I want a family. That's why I created you. I want only goodness for you, dear, dear one. For as wide as one ocean is to the next and the next, and as far as one star is to the next, that's only a portion of My love for you. From eternity to eternity, from the Aurora Borealis to the earth, back to heaven, My love knows no limits, no bounds. My love for you is endless, fathomless, complete, pure and Holy, holy one. From Mary's womb to the Cross, I sent a love letter to you, a precious sweet, soft, and kind little Lamb. His name was written in the stars, yet I sent Him to you because you needed Him. You needed the LAMB OF GOD, and I need you. Until we meet again "beauty-precious," until we meet in the stars, remember, I am with you always, always, always, My lovely one.

Until We meet again ...

In wondrous, mighty love for you, Daddy.

NEED ANSWERS • GOD ANSWERS

• READ OUT LOUD •

Donations toward printing are greatly appreciated
by GloryRealm Productions
email PatriciaGamet@Juno.com